T0146912

MY UNSUNG
SOUL

MY UNSUNG
SOUL

SIX COLLECTIONS OF POETRY AND PROSE

A lyrical journey through life expressed in
six distinctive themes: Love, Nostalgia,
Sorrow, Life, Testimony and Warfare.

DERRICK DERRON HOLLOWAY

MY UNSUNG SOUL
SIX COLLECTIONS OF POETRY AND PROSE

iUniverse books may be ordered through booksellers or by contacting:

iUniverse
1663 Liberty Drive
Bloomington, IN 47403
www.iuniverse.com
1-800-Authors (1-800-288-4677)

Because of the dynamic nature of the Internet, any web addresses or links contained in this book may have changed since publication and may no longer be valid. The views expressed in this work are solely those of the author and do not necessarily reflect the views of the publisher, and the publisher hereby disclaims any responsibility for them.

Any people depicted in stock imagery provided by Thinkstock are models, and such images are being used for illustrative purposes only. Certain stock imagery © Thinkstock.

ISBN: 978-1-5320-2628-7 (sc)
ISBN: 978-1-5320-2629-4 (e)

Library of Congress Control Number: 2017913999

Print information available on the last page.

iUniverse rev. date: 10/24/2017

CONTENTS

Collection One
Reminiscence of Love

Collection Two

Moments of Nostalgia

Collection Three
30/30 Challenge Pieces

Collection Four

Only Poets Say Melancholy

Collection Five

This is Spiritual War

Collection Six

Now Call It Testimony

ACKNOWLEDGEMENTS

I can't begin to acknowledge all the people who've contributed to this journey in some way. There are so many people to thank. In some cases, names have escaped me, but the memories are imprinted on my heart. In other instances, names have been changed or left unspoken, but I thank them just the same for the token of their contributions. So, with those in mind, I say thank you for each smile, each laugh, each tear through all the years of my childhood remembrances. To teachers who wore purple every day, to friendships that were made in second grade, and to girls whose names I can't remember. To Sarah Mary, Ollie Jane Elizabeth, for hands that held me before my footing was sure... my Granny and Grand whose love enveloped me. My Great-Grandfather, Pop, who took me to the barbershop every day and let me play checkers and sip bottles of Nu-Grape. Thanks to Saint John's Baptist Church in Durham, NC for caring for me as a kid. Thanks to Walltown for raising me like you did, and to the West End. Thanks to Naples Place and 2625 Holloway Street, and to the crew of kids who picked on me that first day of riding the bus to school. (I had to slap one of you, but that second day we were cool) Thanks to Lowes Grove Jr. High and the old Southern High School. RIP to my best friends Charles "Chuck" Freeman Hogan III and Franciscus Dixon... too many laughs to remember. Thanks to having one high school sweetheart... for beginning a love affair with poetry. Thanks to all the hearts who came to know and fell for the same lines in love letters that I wrote for all the fellas... (Oops, I wasn't supposed to say that, but we go way back... I think some of y'all still owe me $5) Okay, now seriously... Thank you to my Ex-wife for being a phenomenal mother and raising my amazing son and beautiful daughter. To all my other exes, even the some who live in Texas, I couldn't have asked for better exes than you. Thanks to She and her, and keepsakes and secrets kept, and forsakes, and mistakes, and things I wish I could erase and take back, and change, and do over again... and maybe I'd do some of them the same, and then again, maybe I wouldn't. But each one has gotten me a little closer to where I am now. So, each one was meant to be somehow, and I wouldn't be the same without you. Thank you to Cup of Salvation Deliverance Church for putting in the work to change this heart of mine. Thank you to my Power of the Tongue Family for every poem and rhyme that have inspired me. 4 The Kingdom, Andra Kellon, Charles V Freeman III and Franklyn Miller, thank you for every word of Spoken Word I heard my life in. To my Spiritual Beasts Family keep on writing. To the love of my life, my wife, my queen... Sabrina Holloway, thank you for ever being supportive of me in everything I dream and pursue. I love you. To my Mother and Father, I wouldn't be who I am today if not for your raising me the right way... I shall not depart from it. To my Lord and Savior, Jesus Christ, I give the honor and glory for my life, and for the rest of my life. Amen.

FOREWORD

I have written under a number of hats on topics that span the spectrum, and I can't confine my mind to one set of rules by which to write my life, so I let go in this poetic journey.

The themed collections here are mere glimpses back over the course of my life, from childhood to heartache and from sin to salvation. Every part to tell its part of my heart. Confessions and lessons learned through ways of love, loss and loneliness. Experiences gained through error and pain, and testimonies from the same mistakes made repeatedly. Joys of yesterdays and yester ways, and brighter hopes for tomorrows. The sorrows of losing friends and loved ones... the burdens of shame... are all written in the same name of The Unsung. Each one a song silenced in my soul. My Unsung Soul.

Maybe you'll get to know me on a more intimate level, and maybe you'll see yourself in these memories, but in either case I hope the places you will go on this journey into my soul bring you closer to exploring your own. I hope you laugh at me and remember being as young as we were then when you read a nostalgia piece. I hope you'll identify with a sinner's cry and need to find release. I hope you'll be swept away in beauty and betrayed at the same time when you read the story between the lines. If I can't translate the gamut of emotions that overcome us, I must continue to try until I am dust. Ashes to ashes... from past to passage ways we are created for a length of days called this lifetime. Come, and take a journey through mine. ~ The Unsung Poet

DEDICATION

To Kelcey Nichole, KenDale Jermaine and LaTrelle Marquise...
The best parts of me.

REMINISCENCE
OF LOVE

LOVE

One could exist in such a place as this an entire life and be satisfied in its confines. There exists no freer place than in the space between the lines. I hide myself away in here. My dreams have never seemed as clear as the moments I've spent lost in you. I would lose myself in you time and time again, not giving a care to the hours I spend, nor the days that drift away... Nor for the years that I will never regain, or for having been called a fool. For being in love is all I know of the time I'm lost in you. No cares nor regrets for loneliness... No memories of discontent. Though heartache becomes my habitat, I find no shame in it. I would share homelessness for shelter, trade happiness for pain, and wander waywardly in memory to be lost in you again. Love.

S.A.B.R.I.N.A.

To the Tenth Degree

Sweet angelic being...
Resonating innocent nuances astonishingly...
She's able bodied reverence in Namaste adoration...
Subtleness and brilliance
Reverberating in natural alliance...
Such a Beauty rarely is naturally ascertained.
She, appreciation beholden recognition,
Implicitly never allows.
Soaring above bravery releasing inhibitions
Nefertiti avowed.
So amazing... Blessed restoration
Indispensably needed always...
Sensitivity amplified by resounding intimacy
Nurturing assuredness.
Subliminally aware... Blindly recognizing intrinsically.
Naturally astounding.
Serenity abounding...
Beloved relatively inevitably...
Necessity accentuated.

She's made to Be Magnified in My Eyes...

TEACH ME HOW TO LOVE YOU

Teach me how to hold you...
How to fold you in these arms
So you'll know that you're secure
And ever safe from any harm.
Teach me how to respect you...
How to listen when you speak
How to talk to you... and understand...
How to learn the things you teach.
How to comfort you
How to caress you
How to confront you with the truth
How to believe in you
How to receive from you
How to accept the things you do
Teach me what it means when you're silent...
How it seems when you're sad
What to say to calm your anger
What not to say to make you mad.
How to assuage your frustrations
How to ease your fears
How to take away your insecurities
When to wipe away your tears...
When just to let you cry
When all you need is time
When there's nothing I can say
To bring you peace of mind.

Teach me the things that make you weak
So I'll know how to make you strong.
Teach me the things that caused you hurt
Before I came along.
Teach me why you feel the way you feel
When you feel the way you do
So I'll know how to heal the way you feel
When you're feeling blue.
Teach me what it sounds like when you're happy
So I'll know your voice of joy.
Teach me what each smile means
So I'll know when you're being coy.
Teach me how to touch you in the ways you want me to.
How to caress you in the night when your day is through.
Teach me how to place no one and nothing above you.
Teach me how to be your man.
Teach me how to love you.

Natural Beauty Haiku

Her Beauty's captured
Not in locks of flowing curls
But Essence alone.

Luna Haiku

Beheld in bright eyes
Heavenly light in night skies
Harvest moon rising.

Elemental Love

Come Oasis...
Take me places where cool waters reside.
Unto pools of you, hide me inside.
As I take the way of hardened clay...
Make moist and mold my shape.
Hold my copper toned torso in arms of ebony embrace.
Make dew weep from me like branches of willow trees...
Blow over me slowly like wind strewn leaves
Softly come to know me.
Be free; Let flow thee... waves of love to be made...
Glaze me till we glisten
While we listen to the whispers of our escapade.
Give way to your desire like wild fire upon fields...
Let it carry you every way the wind turns.
Lay still under my hand like sun beaten sand...
Feel how the earth beneath us burns...
A blazing passion... A brazen love...
Embellished with a twisted kiss of forbiddances...
Sigh as I part thy lips.
Sinks in my Soul like seas sank ships.
Delve deep into this abyss of sinful bliss...
Come savor this erotic tryst.
Her treasure no longer hidden...

A pleasure forbidden found...
Caught in a drift of love as we flow down.
My fire, my water, my earth... the air I breathe...
Her love becomes reverent to me.
Ever meant to be... Elemental Love.

AS I COME TO KNOW YOU

I hear the sound in your voice when you speak to me.
I see the look in your eyes when it's me you see...
And they say to me that this woman "knows you" in some way.
In a way that's to others unbeknown...
So, at times I wonder, from where have you come to know me?
From how far and for how long have you traveled to me?
In what past life did we first meet?
And of us two, who did first speak?
And I remember things you would not believe...
Times you would count as dreams...
A touch felt and kisses shared underneath the willow trees.
Now as I come to know you,
I remember things such as these...

A life with you in a placid blue
Where we flew in a liquid sky...
And loved in a water garden of life,
In a world of you and I...
Bound by no place, nor space, nor time,
We gently drift streams in the abyss of yours and mine...
Tails twisting as we embrace...
Flowing swiftly in a current of love...
Bare torsos glisten in a rippling shimmer
As we explore the world above.
Dive with me into Destiny,
And share with me the bluest sea's...

In the truest love you've ever dreamed...
As I come to know you.

I remember a clearing in a wood where we would often meet.
As I prance on golden hoofs you danced on naked feet.
And you caressed me...
And wrapped your arms around my neck...
And laid your head upon my chest... And you mounted me,
So I could know the feeling of your flesh upon my flesh.
And I ran, and you rode with the wind in our hair.
Upon angel's wings we would ascend to trod a clouded air.
Our lover's flight into night would bring a lover's moon.
We'd return unto our secret wood,
Knowing morning would come soon.
And you'd rest with me beneath the willow trees...
Listening to lovebirds call...
Beside a wooded stream, under the forest greens...
Behind the waterfalls.
As I come to know you...
I remember the sound of a cracked whip,
And the feel of a master's thrash...
How you looked upon me while he ripped the skin upon my back.
And I remember you holding our child...
How the tears filled your eyes...
And how you shuttered with my every agonizing cry.
For what cause must so great a price I pay,

Than but to die for the life I made?
Made to suffer for the love I gave...
Though boldly you confessed your love for me,
I was still a slave.
In their eyes, nothing purifies the sin of mixed blood
Except shed blood...
There is no cleansed black skin but a dead one...
So, made you to choose the life that would lose,
And see the price that he would pay.
To save the life of the one we made,
You gave my life away
And set me free with the choice you made...
But my love was still a slave... And ever will it be the same...
As I come to know you.

Missing You

From a series entitled: Between the Lines

It's been so long since words were spoken between us. How I've missed so much, the times we would lay and talk into the night. Till the night became day and the room became bright. I reminisce good mornings we would share getting ready... how I laid there watching you dress. Silly now to confess, that room was a sanctuary to me. It should have been mine... In my mind, it's still a place of rest that I find. It should be ours even now. Here, I have only solitude. This room holds no perfumes. Its fragrance is just air; it holds not the scent of you. Its walls haven't been touched by the sound of your laughter. There are no secrets tucked in its corners, no kisses shared upon its floors. It's just a hollow space behind closed doors... A place where I spend little time.

It hurts to say I miss you, but I do. You have no idea how much, and I can't explain. So, simply know that though I hurt... and sometimes I'm lost for words, I'm also dealing with the pain. One day I'll be over you, "sew it seams", but not today...

You linger on the outskirts of my life, touching me like threads of a web. I can't see you, but I always know you're there. With everything in me, I believe that you love me. That belief at times is such a hindrance to me that I'd rather not believe... My mind torments me to believe that your staying close to home was meant to give me hope, but most times it proves me wrong and hopeless. My mind finds no rest. How many tests does love put one through? How many memories must I endure... of the time last we made love? Let me recount the ways of...

I only fill the pages... fill the pages with conversations I've had with inanimate you's. How silly of me to speak to empty spaces... places where you should be. How hopeless of me... knowing pillows don't speak. Hints of perfume fade away and photos blur under tears after all these years. To look at you, I simply close my eyes. Whispering your name brings you no closer my way, but the sound of it soothes me when I say..."D'ever a hearTlesS liar, all rave at her desires"

For some silly reason, my traitorous heart for treason... made me kiss your lips one night while you were sleeping... now every night I'm missing you.

BROKEN RECORDS

I'm not ready to deal with another person's insecurities. I'm not ready to persuade another person's pains away. I'm not ready to be scrutinized through the eyes of someone who can't seem to see past their last... so; maybe I'm not ready for you. I'm not ready to have to explain myself to someone else. I'm not ready to be criticized for something I did that made you feel insignificant. I'm not ready to drop what I'm doing so that you can feel you have my undivided attention. I thought that I should mention that maybe; I'm not ready for you. I'm not ready to have to convince you that there's no need to compete for me. I'm not ready to have to deal with your jealousy. I'm not ready to go through "How do I know I can trust you?" So, maybe I'm not ready for you. Though I'm always accountable, I'm not ready to have to account for my whereabouts. I'm not ready to have to say "I've been here and I've been there." I'm not ready to be put through background checks and inquisitions, because you feel I refuse to share. I'm not ready to be prodded and preyed upon for something that you want, that I'm not ready to give. I'm not ready to create a trusting relation that you're not ready to let live... so, maybe I'm not ready for you. Maybe......... or maybe it's the other way around?

I Understand, But Why?

From a series entitled: Between the Lines

I understand that you've been hurt in the past,
But I wasn't the one who hurt you...
I understand that your trust has been broken,
You've been misled and openly lied to,
But I wasn't the one who deceived you... or tried to.
I understand that you've been taken for granted by a man,
Thought less of than your true worth, and you hurt...
But I wasn't the one who neglected you...
I never subjected you to anything less than my best.
I understand that you've been taken advantage of,
But I wasn't the one who took advantage of your love...
I wasn't the one who used you...
I understand that you've been bruised too,
But I wasn't the one who abused you...
I understand that you've built walls
To conceal hurts and hide fears behind...
I understand your hearts guard's been fortified...
I understand that you're not trying to take the chance
Of being hurt again,
But you need to let love in.
I understand frustration seems insurmountable
When you hold yourself accountable
And recount the mistakes you've made and the debts you've paid...
And have then to do all that you can to warrant against
Making the same mistakes twice.

On guard, is your life...
I understand the insecurities that come with any failed relationship
Fault or no fault of your own...
I understand enduring a pain that seems to last too long...
And what it is to long to be rid of regrets...
Wishing you could forget...
Wishing it never happened, but constantly remembering that it did...
I understand how hard it is to make the decision to forgive...
I understand but... let me ask you this...
Why should I be the one who suffers for the mistakes that he made...? Punished for the hurts that he gave...?
Why should I have to live with your lack of trust
For the lies that he told...?
When I've told none of my own...
Why should I have to break through barriers that you built
In fear of his using you...?
When all I ever do is prove to you...
That you're not in this alone...
Why should I have to deal with your "who is she" insecurities
Because of his infidelity...?
And why am I compared to every idiot
Who failed to recognize your worth...?
When I recognize you first...
Why can't you see me through new eyes the way I do you...?
Don't get me wrong...

If I have to heal you in order to have someone worth holding on to,
I'll do it...
Because there's a passion behind those fears that longs to be
relinquished.
I see a "she" that longs to be released.
There's still a love that lives inside that bruised and broken heart,
And if I have to give twice as much as he did to have it, I will...
Because all of me times two equals all of me... and you're more than
worth it.
If I have to daily build you into the beautiful woman that I see when
I look at you
Until you see her the same... I'll do it.
Willingly without complaint... until every insecurity is erased.
I'll do it because I can.
I'll do it because I care to fulfill the needs in you.
That's what makes me a Man.

Between The Lines

Will you be my lover?
Will you come and cover me?
Or shall we continue to live between the lines?
Will you be my fantasy?
Or will you be real for me?
Will I ever look deeply into your eyes?

Shall ever, I trace your silhouette with my fingertips?
Shall bated breaths forever wait between our lips?
If kissing a dream means the dream would end...
Would you kiss me or dream our dream again?
Will passion consume us...?
In the moments of our first touch...
Or will we restrain...
The fury of our flames?
Have you ever been taken... into dawn from dusk?
Ever waken to the feeling of a thrust
Tunneling deep inside...
Where two souls collide
In a rhythm like the motion of a wave?
Feel your body break...
Feel the heat of my sands as we dance to the music of our moans.
Feel me fill you full...
As I push you pull...
Till we break upon beaches of our own.
Inhale... quickly...

Exhale... slowly...
Each breath... a closer step to ecstasy...
How deep will you breathe for me?
How deep will you breathe...?
Or will I proceed to take your breath away?
Love is a treacherous cave...
Be free and swept away.
Or love me... and forever be my slave.

Will you give me what I need?
Hear me, on bended knees...?
When I speak secrets into your sacred places?
When you tell me come inside,
Will our two souls as one survive
If I'm the island in the midst of your oasis?
Are you ready for this thing?
For such love I'm about to bring.
Free the fire of your desires; come to life.
It's time you made up your mind.
Endeavor your heart with mine...
Or shall we forever only live between the lines.

Soulmate Part 1
From the series: Between the Lines

I am a victim of love. I'm weak in my affections. I'm trying to hold on to what I see in you. The potential of we... The possibility that there is something in us that's worth more than everything we have to offer individually. What we culminate into is a more valuable thing than each of our individual self-worths. Only in our becoming one is it worth losing ourselves. I'm trying to completely lose myself in you. I'm trying to demonstrate in every way on a daily basis that this is where my place is. I'm trying to show you that I know you by your soul and not just your outer appearance. I'm trying to reach into the depths of you and pull out into existence something that has not thrived. I'm trying to bring alive that empowered she I see inside. I'm trying to trust you with the very fibers of my being... and weave into yours every thread of love... honor... honesty... trust... dignity... respect... chivalry... kindness... peace... hope... gentleness... and compassion... that I can sew into an everlasting tapestry of what we were meant to be. I've been me, alone and lonely for too long and I am only made whole as my completed self by you. How do we two walk as one? What bond or cord must bind us in oneness?

You so often fight against me... when I'm trying to embrace unity with you. Is it fear that stumbles you? Is it a lack of trust or just an unwillingness to believe in love? My strength is wary... My direction is wandering in my wondering if we two will move centrifugally through the curves of love. Will our circle be broken? What can I do to hold in? Is there nothing? Is there something? What? Because I am willing to turn towards love every time, but I find at times I'm losing momentum. I feel my wheels are spinning in one place. Why can't we get past this trial of pace? I walk alone... and only my misery seems to follow me.

I need your strength... your support... your companionship to walk with me... All that I have is vested in you, so if I have nothing left... then myself must do.

We way heavy on my mind at times. My greatest fear is that we won't survive. I can't take losing all that I've found in you. The beauty that I've created in my masterpiece can't be replaced nor erased or painted over. A work of art in progression... my confession of the truest love. A lesson in you is love... and I want to learn from you the essence of all you possess. All that comprises your inner being. Your heart, your feelings, your emotions, your with holdings, your weaknesses and your strengths, your soul and all it holds. You hide from me and think I don't see the cries you try to conceal... all is revealed in love. I read every word that seeps from your soul. Told or untold... nothing is lost to me, because I only long to know you. I would recognize you by scent if my eyes ever failed me. By touch, by kisses and fingertips... by your auras' evanescence and the essence of your femininity.

I just want you to trust me. Trust that we will be everything that I believe. I see it in us... our love is not such that is easily broken. It was spoken into destiny. Confessed into existence... believed into being and received completely in me. I am our loves visionary. The clearest thing I've ever seen in my mind's eye is you and I. I would be blind to love if you were not the extension of my soul. I love to the exponential power of infinity times itself. The sum of my love is the equivalent of cosmic implosion. Time folding into itself... it transcends and extends beyond every unit of measurement... its construct is elemental... unalterable... it will never falter nor cease to be. It is Always.

You Move Through Me

You move through me
Like whispers of a distant love...
A kindred spirit's reminiscent touch
Reverberating in my soul in such...
A manner as could n'ere be told.

You rise and swell in my chest...
As I breathe rose scented breaths of what's left in hints of you.

Scents of you... embedded in my pillow
Silhouettes in silken linen
Kisses teasing the beginning of my day,
My... "As We Lay", Crazy...Love afternoons,
Stolen moments run amiss with my thoughts of you.

You move through me
With good intentions,
But interventions were intended for such a taste as this.
I can't wait to kiss.
Nape first, and then this...
Let me whisper secrets to your silent places.

Come nigh, be my Oasis.
Come again, and come soon.
I'm addicted to the waters of your love.
My come down from above,

My must have been sent from heaven...
Cause every moment I spend with you is a blessing.
My confession, yes, is this...

You move through me

Like life...
The blood I bleed, the air I breathe, the water I need, the song I sing.
Like passion coursing through my heartbeat
I race for you.
My taste for you, a sweet addiction...
I fiend for Innervisions.
My dreams bid me stay away with you.
When you're next to me...
My wakened dreams are true.

You move through me.

Serenade

Bend my ear
With words like notes of jazz...
Tell me the things I long to hear.

Sing me a song
Of soft surrender...
Come near to me, come near.

Play on my heart-strings like piano keys
The melodies of my love sing of only loss.
Return to me, like a new day.

Seren a de`. Seren a de`.

Let me listen with content,
Serendipity meant for me,
As you confess a love relentlessly.

Bend my ear with words I long to hear.
Sing to my sorrows like violin strings...
Yield your bow gently.

Be sparing for my despair.
My cares weep away reluctantly.
Sing to me serenity.

Seren a de`.

Kisses in the Wind

Like feathers released on a breeze,
Wondering where they'll float to,
I blow you... kisses in the wind.
To be caught and sent again
Like messenger doves.
Breathed like breath from heaven above.
Savored like tastes on the tip of your tongue...
And felt like the touch of love.
Take this...
For ole time's sake kiss
Let's make this unforgettable.
It would be regrettable
If we let this chance slip away...
When just one kiss away
From finding something heavenly.
Fly away to ecstasy
And let this kiss be defined as destiny.
Like a note... in a bottle on the sea,
Send this kiss back to me
Blowing in the wind.

48 Shades of Black

I've watched sunsets and sunrises
That would bring tears to the eyes
Of any soul witnessing such splendor for the first time.

I've seen fields of lavender,
Forests of evergreen,
Lakes so clear the reflection of heaven could be seen in them
Like mirrors laid flat upon the earth,

But I have beheld nothing more beautiful
Than the soft glisten and warm glow of brown skin
In the twilight of a night sky
Under the mystique of a full moon.

I've seen blue seas and white sands,
Trees with leaves colored as vivid as a child's imagination.
I've seen diamonds, emeralds, rubies and gold,
But for me there is no color more precious to behold
Than the forty-eight shades of a black woman.
From opal to onyx,
She comes in an array that places rainbows to shame.

I've felt the earth tremble,
Seen storm clouds roll,
Heard thunder rumble and oceans roar,
But there is no force more commanding

Than the allure of her beautiful brown frame.
Black Woman how I love thee...
Let me count the ways

My Eastern Star... my Daughter Moon...
My Venus... my Isis... my come back soon...
My storm ... my fire... my Tempest Queen...
My take me higher than I've ever seen...
My heaven on earth... my Eden... my Eve...
My forbidden fruit... and my forbidden tree...
My knowledge of good and evil...
My lust... my sin...
My take me over... my come within...
My passion... my desire... my soul on fire...
My quench me with the waters of your love...
My raging rapids...
My river... my flood...
My giver... my love...
My lover... my friend...
My we were, when we should have never been...
My seductress... my mistress...
My adulterous affair...
My scarlet letter A that I'll forever bear...
My just had to have you... my I'll never tell...
My rendezvous... my secret... my know you so well...
My flirtation... my temptation... my fantasy... my dream...
My wife... my life... my everything...

GOOD MORNING HEARTACHE

I woke up this morning feeling some kind of way
A sentimental mood playing in the back of my mind
Reminiscent thoughts and memories of a time
Where we once weren't so distant.
And the instant I opened my eyes
I realized the vision of you fading away and...
It was just a dream
Faces and places I hadn't seen
In years started to reappear and...
It felt dearer to me now than it did then.
Those old emotions started to spin...
Like merry-go-rounds in the playgrounds of my mind
Found myself drifting back in time for a moment's sake
Wondering still if it was just a mistake
Or was it worth all the pain we gave?

GOOD MORNING LOVE HAIKU

We once wed to be
Now, wake each day happily
To love the morning

YOU WERE MADE FOR ME

And Created He Woman

I can imagine His hands
Carefully molding the clay that shaped you
Delicately draped you in Beauty
Glazed you in Godiva tones
After taking you from bone of my bone

I can imagine I lay sleeping...
The only thing to keep me from weeping
In awe of your magnificence
Created in my presence
From the very essence of His glory
And formed in reverence right before me
Would have been too much
So, placed me to sleep with slightest touch
And as I awake
You take my breath away.

THINKING OF YOU

Rewind these dreams and scenes
That play over again in my mind
Refine memories lost to me in time
Resign from vapor chasing visions I've hasted away
Each day I wasted away in rhyme.

Haunted by thoughts of you I dare to share
Even with myself
The things unseen that I've shared with no one else
Moments spoken into existence in the corners of my mind
Where I've hid your face to seek a thousand times

What good would my heart do to deny you?
What other than destiny could my soul tie to?
What part of living must I be willing to die to
That I might find the will to try to goodbye you?

Battlefields of love lost I cross for mere glimpses sake
Another journey into uncertainty I'll certainly make
My traitorous heart is a risk I'm willing to take
For brokenness is a constant state of break
And I'm unafraid to break again
Forsaken destiny for the place I'm in
My soul cries for soteria from these soul ties
I wept wisteria tears for distant years
I hear synonyms of your name that speak Earth

I think first of Heaven, when I think of you
Maybe away you should have stayed from shooting stars
For my heart the scars have only started to fade
How many hearts have I traded for taking yours?
Some doors were never meant to be opened

But walking through opened doors
At the end of dark hallways is a given
Being drawn in wasn't our decision
What other choice did we have?
When you smiled, I laughed...
When you hurt, my heart bore the pain...
And when you breathed, my rhythm was the same
And you lived in the swell of my chest
Now my mind finds no place to rest
For thinking of you

NOTHING EVEN MATTERS

As Inspired by Lauryn Hill and my Wife

I could erase all the mistakes we'd ever make
And take away all the hurts we ever gave
And save the sorrows of our tomorrows
But it wouldn't mean a thing
Because the going through with you
Is what brings meaning
And nothing even matters to me...
There's no place I'd rather be
Than somewhere with you beside me
And where doesn't make a difference
As long as the experience that we share there
Is represented with love and care
Nothing even matters...

If we were adrift at sea
And surrendered to the breeze
I could just as easily be pleased
Spending lazy river afternoons with you
With nothing more to do than to...
Gaze into the abyss of you.
And time won't even matter...

Our years will bring tears and laughter
Enough to fill each chapter with memory verses
Of for betters and worses...

Blessings and curses

And none will ever matter
A moment longer than the latter...
Cause nothing even matters but you.

Life was meant to be spent...
And if must I give it
Let me live it willingly with thee
Where nothing even matters to me...

But I Want You Anyway

Collision Infinity

It's not news that you're no good for me.
It's not news that we were never meant to be.
It was a travesty waiting to happen.
And I can only imagine
What could've been between us
If only sin hadn't come in between us
Like I knew that it would...
I saw it coming
Like a collision in slow motion
Between two unstoppable forces
But intentions have to play out their courses
Whether good or bad
And it seems the only choice we ever had
Was to collide like implosive anomalies
Creating black holes in our souls
I really don't want to live without you
But being pulled in will be the end of me.
It was over when I could begin to see
Blurred lines between us...
No point in fighting anymore
The feelings we've been unwilling to explore.
There's nothing else to say...
We both know where this is going
We should stop
But I want you anyway...

Why should I regret you?
Why should I be made to forget you?
I should have been the one to first beget you...
Now I wish I'd never met you
I wish this heart had never let you
Create new places to explore
If I could go back to the "day before" the day before
I ever knew you
And erase all the pains that would come through you
I wouldn't choose to
I'd just walk us through another door
And if they told me we were doomed from the start
I'd turn to you and say...
I know
But I want you anyway

ALL THAT MATTERS NOW

Laying in my arms...
The softness of your skin under my fingertips.
The feel of your kiss upon my lips.
I lay awake and wonder while you slumber.
Will you lay with me a year from now?
But you're here now
And maybe I should consider it enough
To have your head rest upon my chest
And to feel your touch.
If tomorrow you wake and walk away
My life today... would be no less fulfilled
Than had I lived a million years.
Because inside the moments we've shared
I've love a lifetime... And I find
That only the moments matter.
You're here now and maybe it should be enough
To close my eyes and feel your touch...
And think only this moment matters.
I could anguish my heart with thoughts of tomorrow
Reminisce past heartbreaks sorrow
Or beware of how much I care...
But what good would it do me now?
Because without a doubt you're here now...
And that's all that matters.
You're here now... and now it's just enough
To hold you close and be in love...
Only the moments matter.

All in Love is Fair

As Inspired by Stevie Wonder

All is fair in love
There are no rules to win or lose
It's just a game played by fools
For truths and dares n'ere would do
For parts played by our hearts
For secrets sake... for words never said
For thoughts that laid there in my head
For hallowed halls and if walls could talk
Oh, the stories they would tell
If absence makes the heart grow fonder
My hearts a prison cell
No wanders beyond these four walls
No yonders behind these bars
Just silhouettes of solitude and a sentimental mood
But memories are all they ever are...
Who's ever held a memory?
Arms have never said remember me...
Their longing is only to hold again
To enfold within where embrace begins
And forever is in never letting go
There are no rules to this
Loss was the cost of a kiss
And I've paid for every mistake I've made
If losing was the only chance in choosing
I probably still would have played
All in love is fair

A Poetic Love Affair

She carries me
Carries me through nights of quiet desperation
Into early mornings
Where only interpretations of her
Play subliminally in my mind
Her sublime affections define
The very essence of our being

Seeing her before me in rare display
Her bare form lay upon my sheet
And we are a never ending love affair
I and Poetry...

Made her my mistress
To kiss
Pen tips as lips
To pages
She assuages my need to feed
And I hunger for her nightly
I write She
Comes to me
We sated embrace the day awaited
But lately she seems distant

Reminiscent
We've drifted apart

Her stops come before my starts
And there stare blank pages between us
I need she redeem us...

It seems frustrations weigh as heavy
As waters against the levee
Overflow my Soul
The weight of the world upon my shoulders
I long to hold her to a higher standard
Her hand commands my words
Through heartbreaks of silences ever heard
Echoing in my soul

She insights me to speak
In passionate peaks of poetic ecstasy
With wetted tip my quill leaks
Ebony upon her ivory
Heavily upon her heart
We swept away into hours of dark
Until dark become the day
Indelibly she lay upon me
Given sanctuary upon my chest
She rests...
In our poetic love affair

MOMENTS OF NOSTALGIA

A Toast: To Lil Brothers

Dedicated to Terrence Jermaine Holloway

We used to be like nobody's business...
Tight... like puckered lips sucking on lemons.
We was always together
I couldn't have left you if I wanted to
You stuck to a Brother like glue...
Like bubblegum on hot sidewalks.
We used to talk about everything that made sense to
Six year olds...
Like how to catch bees, bugs and tadpoles.
Climbing trees and how old you had to be
To go to 2nd Grade?
I remember back in the days
When we played in city parks
When hop-scotch was still cool for dudes
When we didn't know any better,
But we knew better than to not to do as told.
You must've been bout 4yrs old
Dragging that stuffed dog around...
Half the fights I got in was over you.
"Take ya Brother witcha" was just a phrase, I got use to
Till I wouldn't have it any other way.
"Let's go Bro... C'mon Jay"
"Where we going?" was your favorite thing to say.
To the park to play ball
Or to the mall to "chase squirrels"...

It was me and you, Babyboi, against the world.
Like Wally and the Beaver...
Or more like Arnold and Willis Jackson
We had Different Strokes for folks back then.
Picking pears and shaking pecan trees to sell by the bag
Wishing we had a wagon...
Watermelon on the porch at Gran's
Saving the seeds... Trying to grow a watermelon tree.
Tying strings to the legs of June bugs
To hear 'um make that sound
When we'd whirl and twirl the string around...
Found Mama scared to check our pockets
When she washed clothes; could be anything...
From dead snakes to shoe strings...
I mean... We were Boys!
Our toys were different...
But I'd let you hold a toy or two.
Cause you tried to do the things you saw me do.
But, Man you was destructive!
You must've chewed a hundred army men...
But you never got mad cause I didn't let you win
You just played harder...
That was the start of when "you got game"
And through the years I watched you rise to fame.
I'm proud of you Lil Bro. More than you'll ever know.
Those tag-alongs play like my favorite songs

From back in the day.
And I didn't want to neglect to say...
I'm so glad I grew up with you.
Here's to you...
I love you, Babyboi

Happy With What We Had

Bo-Bo's... They make your feet feel fine
Bo-Bo's... They cost a dollar 99
Bo-Bo's...
Yeah, I remember wearing the low top Chuck Taylor's without the star
The ones piled high in the center aisle bin at the Roses and K-Mart.
New shoes...
We couldn't wait to get um'!
"Take off yo school clothes and put on yo play clothes"
Every day when we came in the door after walking home from school
House smellin' like spaghetti.
Whole neighborhood playing in our front yard.
And my Gran...She'd try to feed every one of um'
(She never knew who wouldn't eat that night)
She just shared what she had.
We all did back then
Back when kids were glad to share with a friend
Back when...kids played outside.

(Running in the house screaming)
"Graaaaaan! ......Mr. Joe brought you a bushel of greeeeeen beeeeans!"
Out of breath...
Breathing hard.
"He said, you ain't gotta give him no money, he just won't some of yo sweet-corn"

And this...
This was the norm.
This was the reason everybody's kitchen was painted the same color green
Cause when you had more than you needed
You didn't have to think hard
To think of someone who needed...
Some.

Yeeeah...
We wore our shorts above the knee
And our socks above the calf
If we wore socks...
They'd slouch down around our ankles from stretching out the tops
But we put on a fresh pair every day.
And we were happy with what we had...
Nappy headed happy
Back in the days where you couldn't smack a smile off a child's face at Christmas
Back when stretched out tube socks made the best Christmas stockings
And apples and oranges in a brown paper bag were still considered a treat
We had clothes on our backs and shoes on our feet
And people kept each other fed
And little brothers didn't have any qualms about sharing a twin bed

When bathwater could be used by both of us
If it won't too dirty after the first
And our Sunday's Best was exclusively what we only wore to church.
Hand-me-downs lasted generations
Cause it was new to you when it was your turn
And Sunday school taught us the best lessons we ever learned.

Our fitted sheet didn't match our top sheet
But who knew sheets were supposed to match?
And sometimes my favorite part of the jacket
Was the patch...
We were happy playing with a flat ball and a metal trashcan
In a backyard of dirt with our best friends
We had no idea we were poor.
Kids just aren't that thankful anymore
Their sense of entitlement today is sad
Remember...
When we were happy
With what we had?

DAYDREAMING

Qasida

I want to paint a picture for you
Give you visions of brand new
Dance in your imagination like I used to
Give you lucid dreams and things
Take you places you've never seen
Awaken fantasies you'd never believe
Travel places and spaces beyond time
I wanna ride merry-go-rounds inside your mind
Have you sliding down rainbows and catching shooting stars
I wanna wake up on Venus and go to bed on Mars
I wanna sail away on summer afternoons
Through cotton candy clouds in hot air balloons
To land on a (dessert)ed island
Build castles of sugar sand
And swing the day away in a hammock hand in hand
I wanna stroll across the ocean
Feel the motion of waves under our feet
Ride on backs of blue whales across the sea
I wanna fly away
Over hills of golden hay
Land in fields of lavender and evergreen
Spend a lifetime in a land of dreams
Where nothing is what it seems
Where we can live off of wishes and make believe
Chocolate kisses and fruit trees

51

Sleep in tree-houses grown from magic beans
Where the sun never sets, but always rises
And we wake up each day to new surprises
Humming birds and singing bees
Flying fish... Talking trees
And walking instruments make up marching bands
Where everyone understands
Going over the waterfall
Is a must for all
But nothing is mandatory
Except for bedtime stories
And there's no such thing as scary
So every tale is fairy
Every ending is merry
Like Christmas and never a Halloween
Shadows are never seen
Trees never lose their leaves
And of course all of the horses have wings
I wanna spend just a little time
Exploring the boundaries of your mind
Come and run away in the rhythm of a rhyme
Let's get lost in the moment
Time was never meant
To spend every minute thinking of the meaning
So, let's spend some time daydreaming

PROGRESS

Class is in session.
It's a valuable lesson.
Let's see how far we've come
Since the Great Depression.
There's been a constant progression
In our downfall,
And we say we've made progress.
But let's put that theory to the test...

I would give back the years
If we could flash back in time
For fashion's sake.
Back when men dressed like men
And women didn't have to take off everything
Just to make a statement.
Back when staying out late meant
You still made it home at a decent hour
Rather than leaving home at an hour
Where few things decent are being done.
Just look how far we've come
From the Class we had when we first begun...

Sometimes I wonder
Where those "back in the day" values went.
Back when pay was spent taking care of business
Because we had business owner mentalities

Paid for through the fatalities of
All the generations that came before us.
Now we stand in chorus lines for handouts
Singing for our supper
Thinking we never had the upper hand.
But we're content with being given the underhand...

And if you can't over stand that statement
You'll keep standing under it
Waiting for someone else to come uncover it.
I hope you discover it for yourself...
We can't rebuild our wealth working for someone else.

What happened to the movement
Where we inspired a renaissance and were the affluent?
Artists and Authors... Performers, Painters and Poets...
To look at us now we'd never know it
If it hadn't been written and history made.
Just look how we've repaid
The debts that were already paid
All for the sake of saying we've made progress.

And I must confess...
There has been some positive change.
But compared to what we've lost, what have we gained?
Our ancestors would be ashamed...
Look what we've done with what they left us
To where we've come since they blessed us
With being overcomers.
I'm overcome...with distress about this mess
That we call Progress.

Barbershop Chairs

Few truths are told like those shared in these chairs
These chairs where few truths are told.
And I remember those days of old...
Sitting on stacks of phonebooks
Spinning round in that big ole rotating chair
Just a nappy headed happy child
Without a care in the world
Putting make believe cream on my face
Pretending I was getting shaved
Straight razed like the old timers used to
Sipping on a Nu-Grape
And eating Now-&-Laters by the bag full
Maybe a Moon Pie or two
Waiting on Mr. Liles to pull that lever on the chair
To raise me up higher in the air
So I could see myself in the mirror.
Listening to conversations float over my head
They would say what he said she said
While I would play checkers
Monday morning hecklers who smoked for breakfast
Joked religion, fishing and politics
Sunday morning hypocrites
Throwing their heads back to sip communion wine
Like it was a shot of Jim Beam's finest.

Even as kids, we laughed at this... Now I reminisce
Names of characters I couldn't begin to make up
Names like Toeless Joe, Hambone, Buster and Spunk
Names who never thought they'd be remembered
In some poet's poem about barbershop chairs.

My Brother's Keeper

Now "we" prefer our faces be looked upon independently
So "he" won't be mistaken for "I"
We accentuate our identity rather than be
Looked upon indiscriminately
We collectively refuse to be our brother's keeper
So eye turn blind I's and keep to myself
Become the staples of our self help
Because "I" only helps "myself"
And "he" can't have what "I" has
Even when there's more than enough
So "we" are perpetually stuck in keeping up
With the Jones'... (Jones)ing to outdo each other
Cause only one of us can have the upper hand
And "I" won't be taken advantage of
If only "he" would love his neighbor as himself
"We" could see a commonwealth,
But then we're giving in to Socialism
Peace isn't prosperous for us... We need conflict
We're born and bred war profiteers
With a bloodlust for dollar signs
With "some of his" and "none of mine" mentalities
What happened to the reality's that we used to see
When "we" believed it took a village to raise a child?
When "we" faced mile-stones in unity
When "we" embraced community
When "we" was the combined strength of you and me
Before it became "he" and "I"
Back when "I" was my brother's keeper

ROCKETSHIPS TO HEAVEN

{You took me riding in a rocket
And gave me a star
And at a half a mile from heaven
You dropped me back down to this
Cold... cold world.

You took me riding in a rocket
And gave me a star
And at a half a mile from heaven
You dropped me back down to this
Cold... cold world.} ~ Stevie Wonder

We laid on skateboards like bobsleds
Racing downhill on city streets
Our chins against our chests'
The sole of our sneakers
Hot against our feet
Push-up pops and freeze pops
Dripped from our lips...
Summer days spent
Sippin' on frozen Kool-Aid
Back when red was our favorite flavor
When chain linked fences
Were meant to be climbed
When we traded in soda bottles for a dime
And a dollar could get a bag full of candy

Pa-pa was the neighborhood handyman
Mrs. Annie's van picked up all the day care kids
And we never needed a school bus
We just... Walked fast enough to be on time
Back when the hood had a neighborly state of mind
Back when belts held our pants up...
Or tore up our behinds
When switch and britches
In the same sentence wasn't gay
It just meant your happy day was at its end
When three strikes meant I told you twice
And I ain't gone tell you again...
When calling friends
Was just a loud noise you made outdoors
When a visit was done in daylight
When you could play-fight
Till the streetlights came on
And ten o'clock meant everybody was home
But we don't play-fight anymore...
Now, we're double locking doors
Hoping a neighbor never knocks on yours
Not for sugar, butter, flour, milk or eggs
Because now an "ask" is just another "beg"
And we don't borrow
So never mind a "pay you back tomorrow"
Please don't even knock on my door

That's just what neighbors used to be for
Now we watch locks and pretend to be cops
Long gone are those yesterdays
When "Yes, Sir" says were common place
When children's space...
Was somewhere out of "grown folks business"
When "Mother may I"...
Was more than just a game
Back before it became "I won't this!!!"
When slang wasn't profane
And we dared to even call a dog a bitch...
I guess it's no sense wishing for latter days
Sadder days seem here to stay...
I'm in mourning for Saturday mornings
We used to wanna play outside
As soon as cartoons were done
Our imaginations would run... Races
Faces covered in dirt and sweat
If you weren't good and tired
Then you weren't done yet
Riding rocketships to heaven...

SOUTHERN COMFORT

Spittin' watermelon seeds
Sittin' on porch swings
Stringin' bushels of green beans and snap peas
Veggies sold out of beds of pickup trucks
Corn ears and silk husks
And pickin' up pecans by the bag full...
Red wagons hand pulled
And takin' turns swingin' on trees...
Suckin' on honeysuckle and Sunflower seeds
Payin' for penny candy from the dime store
With a hand full of nickels
Where jars of pickled everything
Sat on storefront countertops...

Jumpin' double dutch and playin' hop scotch
Shootin' marbles and pickin' up sticks
And... Trix was for kids who had, we ate Kix
Cause silly rabbits didn't matter to Dad
King Vitamin for Captain Crunch
Puffed Oats for Sugar Puffs
And pancakes at Gran's we couldn't get enough of...

Love, like warm buttermilk biscuits
Like hot coco on a snow day
Like wood stoves and fire places
To froze fingers and faces

Like hand stitched quilts and crochet blankets...
Banquets and buffets on Sunday's
And Soul food cookin'...

Hey, Good Lookin' whatcha name is...?
Maaan, she a DIME! and Girl, he FINE!
And you knew it must be Summertime...
Cookouts in public parks and backyard barbeques
Girls in sundresses and open-toe-shoes
And boys will be Boys like rhythm & blues
And love songs were made for these days
Sweet, like iced tea and Kool-Aid
In red plastic cups
Fun, like Slip-n-Slides in swim trunks
Puppy-love, Pic-Nic's and kisses
Holding hands and makin' wishes
On shootin' stars
Backseats in parked cars
And Drive-In movies...

The smell of Pine trees in a cool breeze
Southern seasons and the changing leaves of Fall
Simple Living and thanksgiving for all
Of these... Southern Comforts

THE HAVE NOT'S

There were those days
Growing up
When times were tough
When not so many had any
Of what we thought was enough
But enough
Was what we had to get by
Coming up was abrupt
But hard times made it worth the try
Till the try became the struggle
Felt like I had to shovel mud with a stick
No handle, not even a grip
Ill equipped to get the grip I was after
But that was just a chapter
In this book of Life.

To call it one in the sequence
Would be a con
The consequence of what was done
Goes far beyond
Your chapter two understanding
I've stood under demanding circumstance
And not by chance
I just exhausted the community chest...
My stamina proves the best in confrontation
So I make the situation subliminal

Project what I expect in the spiritual
And physically came up out of the projects
Where begets and forget me not's were ungotten

The have not's were common place
So much so that we had not's to waste
I laced my shoes in half knots
We had not's in our stomachs
And knots on our heads
Some nights we took our have not's to bed
But that fed my ambition
Got in position
And reconditioned my mindset
To get the begot's I had not to get
Forgot the regrets
Started a new chapter
And called it success
Because failure is not an option
And I have not the heart to be content
With more month than money left
When the money is spent
So I'll spend this next chapter wisely
Cause time flies
But it won't deny me
And it won't define me as the have not's...

BACK IN THE DAY
Part 1

I remember those back-in-the-days.
Biscuitville's and Chic-fil-A's.
Golden Coral after church on Sundays...
Those most fun days nostalgically had to be
When hide and seek I used to creep and kiss this chic named Ayisha.
My Grandma used to keep her...
Her and another girl named Sabrina...
They took turns on my see saw...
I seen and saw it all as I recall at an early age.
I started kissing in the second grade;
Mama tried to kick dirt in my game...
But at 15 I reached home base.
That was the summer of my first job.
Went back to school... my swagger hard...
Ruby Tuesday's improved my cool ways.
My school daze were as follow...
Mr. Holloway didn't play.
I had to stay home if the go wasn't known.
To where with whom was the question...
And the lesson...
Another test in... have yo behind home on time.
I'd come to find my curfew... was a curse to... anyone who...
Could stay out past eleven O' two.
And that was two minutes too late
I'd be on... probation.

But I found a way to have my fun.
The rule was changed to either be in or
Stay out,at the midnight hand.
So I became the "see you tomorrow" man.
My brother on the other hand... was grounded for life.
We had to change his name to "can't get right"...
He wouldn't do right, so, (you know) Pop said he had to go.
I stuck around till 18 years old.
That's when he told me something that I'll...
Never "forgit"....
"I taught you to be a man. I don't owe you sh*t"
Not exactly in those words, but (you know) I knew what he meant...
Said from that day on... to act like it.
To come of age I made mistakes...
Growing up was kinda tough.
I had to learn some rough lessons in love...
Mama told me it would happen, but she couldn't tell me when...
But when it did, I thought I'd never play with fire again.
She said "One-a-these-days One-a-these-girl's gone break your heart"...
It seems that Love always starts with a spark,
But fire burns...
It's a lesson we all had to learn.
But it's a blessing to have had the turn.
I turned ten times the average men's times...
But in times I find my mind rewinding...

I sit and reminisce...
Days of my first kiss.
Not that second grade one, but that laid one.
That stayed once... at thirty-two twelve Venus Drive.
When she runs through my mind... it's been but a moment in time.
My yesterdays will last always...
A token of my broken heart... the most unspoken part...
A reminder to always love hard,
Cause it was worth it.
If it hurt... then it was worth the word forgive.
But the hurting you don't have to relive...
Remember back in the days...

I Miss Music

I used to follow music with a religious faithfulness like no other because there were artists that you had to hear, because they didn't put out music every year and the anticipation was more than worth the wait. The quality of their artistry was renown and you knew you wouldn't be let down by some false produced sound passing itself off as music. And I miss it... I miss the days when I couldn't wait to get paid so I could go the record store. I miss the days before "New Music Tuesdays" when rhythm and blues days consisted of artists and bands who didn't lip-synch their lyrics and digitize their instruments and call it musicianship. I used to follow music, but they're not making music anymore.

I used to love Hip Hop. But now it's just a name adopted by a culture cultivated by a monster that lives under your bed. You never see him but he's constantly filling your head with false evidence appearing real and all your FEAR is make-believed. Because he made you believe that all these new so-called "artists" flooding the industry with stupidity and mediocracy were REAL. Hip Hop used to make Hits that were Hot and Tip the Top of the charts with consciousness. Now it's just switching H's for S's and Drip Droppin' a bunch of BS in your subconscious.

Music used to have a standard. You had to be able to SANG and being mediocre talented wasn't enough to make in the game. Now they're just taking a name and making a sound... Faking a talent for a clown captivated audience. It's bigger than Barnum and Bailey's how they can say these "artists" of today are anything more than maybe's. Because maybe they have some talent and maybe they have a sound... and maybe they don't mind being given the image of a clown just to be "Labeled". Maybe... Maybe not...

I'm a Back in the day baby and they be HOT! It's like the industry forgot how they made HITS... they just took the same letters but misspelled it. They used to use a chorus and a verse, a second and maybe a third, a bridge and sometimes a hook. Now they took two lines and a beat, put it on repeat, looped it and got the whole world hooked on stupid... but THIS ISH AINT HITS!!!

I miss lyrics... What happened to wordplay? What happened to the double entendre of back in the day when lyrics would lay like sheets in place of pages to get inside her head? Now it's just "I wanna take you to bed". What happened to the discipline that made you wanna listen to the words of melody? Some songs shall forever be engrained into the fabrics of our brains.

Times have really changed, but every now and then you hear a Jazmine Sullivan and "Forever Doesn't Last Too Long" and hope still lives on for the songstresses of today.
I miss music.

MEMORIES

Remember your first pet? Mine was just a mutt from around the way who stayed in the alley behind the house I lived in. Mixed with some of this and some of who knows what else... often spending days by himself burying bones and playing in dirt. Hobbled and always super happy to see me; as easy as a breeze... tail wagging like hand fans on Sunday mornings...

Remember slurping on frozen Kool-Aid your mama made in Daisy cups? Sitting "Indian-style" too close to the TV while watching Saturday morning cartoons... When afternoons were spent chasing friends and racings rivals to see who was the fastest in the neighborhood... and the day was good if you didn't get in trouble or have to fight for little brother because some other kid took his ball. All in all, they were good days...

Remember waking up early Monday mornings? Mama had your school clothes laid at the foot of the bed. You peeled out from underneath Superman twin sheets in your Aquaman pajamas and make straight for the kitchen. "G'morning Gran" ...she'd be fixing scrambled eggs and pancakes; tell you to go wash your face without ever looking, she'd just keep cooking and you'd go racing off to the bathroom...

Buttermilk biscuits, red eye gravy and hot grits... These were common scents in Southern kitchens that I grew up in. Scuttle buckets of coal beside a cast iron stove kept winters warm and handmade quilts gave more comfort than comforters... Mamas kisses to tucks us in at night... "Mama loves ya, Baby. Okay now, sleep tight".

Remember weekday afternoons walking home from school? Keep Off Grass signs read like invitations to cut through... six city blocks, shortcuts and quick stops at the corner store was what we would do.

Remember streetlights coming on slow like warnings signs telling you it was time to go home? And long summer days that we'd stay outside and play, at least until the porchlight came on... or Mama called you by your whole name...

Childhood games like "Red Light Green Light", Hide-N-Seek and Mother May I? She'd never say why, but you knew she'd hide in the same place every time it was your turn to count... and the secret was out when y'all got caught kissing on the playground.

Remember cray-fishing in the creek? Leaf-boat racing down city streets when fire hydrants flooded curbsides... Mouths wide open screaming "Ice Cream" every time we heard that theme song... Looking for fifty cent all day long, saying "Gran, can I have a quarter?" ... She correcting you, saying "May I". And day after day, I'd stay trying to find Indian-head pennies and four-leaf clovers... I miss those days over everything.

JOURNEY

To Walk a Mile in Her Shoes
Taken, the road less traveled
Beaten, tattered, torn
On long gravel laid dirt roads
These soles worn heavy... Heavy and worn
No shine left on the tips of these toes
Scuffed and scared
These feet weary have seen hard times
But I wouldn't trade these ways for roads with lines
Cause my defining was written in the journey

Crossed the desert sands of barren lands
Over oceans chained and broken these feet bare carried me
To blister and bleed they were made to seed
Cotton fields
But in turn I learned the strength of my heels
And they dug in
Mud covered and burlap wrapped
We paved paths of slave ways to freedom
And when we overcome we praised in dance

Given a fighting chance
We tip toed across lands that never belonged to us
From dawn till dusk to crop share
But we laid a foundation through tribulation
These ways rough and rugged

Are what paid the way
For so many roads we see paved today

What she gave away was priceless
Her life's best years sacrificed for theirs
But Mother's love moved mountains
Her hurts were only motivation
She carried the belief of generations
And her feet never rested easy
So often she'd find her hands and knees be...

Laid before God
She... stayed before God
Prayed before God
Still more hard times would find her
Burden yoked and heart-broken for struggles sake...
Never fearing how much more she could take
She just placed the weight on a sturdy stance...

Never fearing how much more she could take
She just placed the weight on a sturdy stance...
Found the courage to see past her circumstance
And fought for education to better her generation

She boycotted buses
Walked freedoms way in pain
For every mile she traveled it seems only an inch was gained
And every inch was given a length of rope
That eventually choked the life from those who hanged
But... she never lost her hope
And eventually freedom sang a movement

She then to school went
Only to be spat upon, ridiculed and criticized
Tears would stream from her eyes
But she knew she carried the pride of a Nation
Sought elevation through pursuing higher education

Strength and unity would be her mantra
Her community would be her shield
Her fight for the right to yield the knowledge she wields
Her chance to overcome every circumstance
So, through trial and tribulation she advanced
And took roads less traveled.

Remember That

Remember that time when we were kids and we did
What every kid did, like leaving cookies for Santa
Being Casper on Halloween...?
But the Easter Bunny
Was the scariest thing we'd ever seen...
Funny papers or Comics, for them, were a Sunday must
Just like Saturday morning cartoons for us
And blowing out candles really made wishes come true
When we were addicted to pixie sticks,
PEZ and yoo-hoo...
Lived in a land of Lego's, Crayon's and Play-Doh
And who could say no
To a Slinky, Wonder Wheel or Yo-Yo?
It was Nilla Wafers and Animal Crackers before Oreo's
And "Once upon a time" was just how the story goes
Bed time became a scared time to things in the dark
When a dead goldfish could break your heart
Remember that imaginary friend
You went running against the wind with?
That play uncle that gave the best gifts...
Remember putting spit on it and kissing it to the wind?
When you could dust yourself off and get back up again
When kisses made it better
And dishes could never break
Because you only ate on Tupperware plates
Remember second grade pencils?

When stickers and stencils came in packs
And you couldn't wait
To get the prize in the Cracker Jack's
When Apple Jack's and Fruit Loops
Were at the top of the charts
And Tang was how the morning would start...
When capes were made for pajamas and clothes pins
And winters were made for pajamas with the toes in
And then there was that one room in the house you couldn't go in
So you'd just stand at the edge and stick your nose in...
Remember that?
Playing piggy back races... Dirt and sweaty faces
And nobody seemed to mind
It was such a good time
Rubber Duckies and sail boats if you were lucky
Bath times were made for toys that didn't float...
Marbles and Jack Rocks
Hot Wheels and Building Blocks
Spinning Tops and Jack-in-the-Boxes...
When the foxes and the hounds could still play together
It was better
When mud puddles were made to make you wetter
It was understood...
That being attention deficient was never meant for evil
It was a condition of childhood

And we could ask a thousand questions in a day
Like what color's the ocean? Why the sky is blue?
Why girls don't have pee pees like boys do?
Where do babies come from?
Where is Heaven?
What time is 12 O'clock?
You wanna see me climb the tree to the top?
Remember that November
When you didn't have to sit at the kiddy table
Being able to cross the street by yourself
Remember how good it felt
The first time "You did it" and didn't need anybody's help
Your first sense of self worth
Was heard in a commercial that said...
"I'm a big kid now"
And even though Pull-Ups became a thing of the past
You still occasionally wet the bed some how
But thank Mama's for bed pads
And she was never mad bout washing sheets
Remember making Rice Krispy Treats?
Summer camps and S'more's...
Remember knocking on doors and runnin'?
It was all funnin' until someone knocked on yours...
"Let me speak to yo Mama"
"Don't let me have to tell your Daddy!"
"You better get in here and do your chores"

Remember that?... from days back
When ways were more community
And as a people we embodied religion, respect and unity
But now it seems history is doomed to be repeated
Had opportunity, but like we didn't need it,
We acted as if it were just a choice...
The best trick the devil ever played
Was getting us to give away our voice
Remember that.

BACK IN THE DAY
Part 2

My neighborhood was a jewel to me.
Eight inner city blocks were a sight to see
Those inner city blocks was the place to be
Cause we didn't know to be anywhere else
We played tackle in the front yards
Tag in the street
And you could go to anybody's house and eat
It was always something in the kitchen
Old men talking bout fishing
Politics and religion at the barbershop
We'd run all the way round the block
Knockin'... "Can you come outside?"
Taking turns on bike rides and races
Popsicle juice sticking to our faces
Dirt, sweat and tears
If I could just turn back the years
I wouldn't mind
Returning to that time
When neighbors were kind and generous
Back when dinner was
Still served at the table
On Sunday you went to church if you were able
Come Monday you took off yo school clothes
And put on yo play clothes
And the whole neighborhood wore Bo-Bo's
When patches and hand-me-downs came around

They were new to you
Cause you weren't wearing the same clothes you used to

And everybody had a turn
A life lesson we all had to learn
But respect was something we had to earn
Cause Daddy didn't raise no punks
Little brothers slept on top bunks
And sleep overs
The whole room stunk
Because little boys don't wash their feet...
Some things you just shouldn't repeat
Like grades in elementary and what grown folks said
Cause getting in grown folks business back then
Could get you slapped in the head
Back then children knew their places
And stayed out of grown folks faces
It was the basis of establishing order
Husband, wife, son and daughter was the family
Marriage wasn't a calamity
Before they took prayer out of schools
Before little girls were cruel
They were made of sugar and spice
And everything nice
When we said the Lord's Prayer
And knew the Golden Rule.
Back in the day.

NATURALLY HAPPY HAIKU

Hidden emotions
Rest not within a child's heart.
Joyous by nature...

MAMA'S LOVE

If I could bottle it up and keep it forever
I'd carry it with me everywhere
I'd never share
And whoever'd dare asked for any
Would be deemed unfriendly for doing so
I'd never let it go
I'd keep it close so everyone would know
It's my most precious prized possession
And having learned their lesson
Not to ever ask for any
They could once again be considered friendly
Cause this is my Mama's Love...

It's full of hugs and kisses
Shooting star and birthday candle wishes...
It's got all my favorite things in it
All my bedtime and daydreams in it
It's got Sunday afternoons
Saturday morning favorite cartoons
And homemade cookies and ice cream....
It's got tuck me in to sleeps in it
It's got hide and seeks and trick or treats in it
It's got jelly donuts with sprinkles
And it's got CHRISTMAS!!!
It's my first thing on every wish list
It's the Bestest Mama's Love in the world!

It smells so good
Just like Mama's Love always should...
If I could make a candle of it I would
Incense and sandalwood
Peach cobbler and pumpkin pie
Egg nog and no wonder why...
Warm cinnamon milk and gingerbread man's...
And it feels like holding hands across the street
And getting back up on your feet after you fell and scraped your knee
But you didn't cry...
It feels like flying kites across the sky
And no training wheels...
It feels like only Mama's Love can feel
I can't forget it and I never will.
Mama's Love has always been there...
Through every tear through every care
Through every sorrow and pain I had to bear...
Through every triumph and fall
Mama's Love was there through it all
It was there when I never even called...
It just knew to be there
Like magic
Like make believe...

Like sunrises and Magnolia trees
Mama's Love will ever be nostalgia.
Like reminiscent kisses on the cheek
Before I fall asleep
She whispers to me...
"Mama Loves ya"

WALLTOWN'S FINEST

If I could draw you a map of the eight square inner city blocks that I grew up on, nowhere on it would be found the words ghetto or hood. Those blocks were a beautiful place for me as a child. It's only knowing now that having grown up there then meant that we were a part of the under privileged. As kids, we were happy running in and out of broken screened doors that slammed shut behind us each time we raced out of the house. That slam either meant "I'm hooome!" or "I'm going outsiiiide!", because we'd usually exclaim one or the other as the door opened, and in case it wasn't heard, the slam always was.

We'd tromp across yards, jumping over bushes and fences, because even though there were sidewalks, yards were where we played and it just made sense to go from one to the next in the quickest and most efficient direct way possible. "Stay off the grass, Tom Baillet!" was the sound that greeted us at Mr. Morris's yard. Hop through Mrs. Shirley's bushes and run through Tisha's yard to dive over Papa's hedge and we were halfway down the block. Stop to pick sweet honeysuckle that grew over the fence between Papa and Mrs. Black's backyard, because we never cut through her front yard, then just take the alley the rest of the way down the block.

"Hey, where yawl going? To the park?"

"Naw, we going to the school to play ball!"

The dealers had taken over the park, so the city took the goals down. The courts were covered in broken glass, baggies and needles, roaches and cigarette butts. It won't no point in going over there anymore. At least not to play ball. It was just a hangout for thugs and wannabe gangsters, but we'd go over there sometimes just to say hey to some of the older kids we idolized. OJ and JB, Terry, Spunk and Blue... They'd be smoking and drinking and grabbing on the neighborhood chicks. We saw them at church on Sunday, but during the week they were busy hustlin'. Rarely were any two of them out of lock up at the same time, so sometimes the park was like a family reunion. We'd all get a street football game going from time to time. That's the only time the older kids didn't mind playing with us.

"Give me my brother's ball back!"

I think the fact that we'd get a really bad snow every 5 years or so, is what made such a distinct age gap between the kids in our neighborhood. Mostly boys, but there was a set 4 year gap between the groups. You had the babies, 1 to 4yrs, then it was the 8 to 12's and then the 16 and up boys. Well, I'm 4yrs older than my baby brother and I had to take him everywhere. So, I fought a lot. Especially against the older kids. But they learned not to mess with my brother.

That's just one of a thousand memories I could replay of growing up in Walltown. And maybe I'll write them all down some day, because the truth is, sometimes the memory of a thing is so much better than the reality of it.

I drove through that old neighborhood today. I'm sad to say that not much has changed. It used to be a beautiful place.

LAZY SUMMER AFTERNOONS

Lackadaisical ways
laid-back lazy days
got me reminiscing
sipping on frozen Kool-Aid in Daisy cups
Nutty-Buddy's and Push-ups
Pop Rocks and Pixie Sticks
and how many licks does it take to get
to the center of a Tootsie Roll Pop?

Got me listening to the tunes
of those old
vinyl swooners
music
that was way before my time
but stays in my mind
cause I'm
just a back-in-the-day-kind-a-fella

Play me some Ella
or some Sarah Vaughn
Ms Fitzpatrick was magic
but I loved the tragic life of Lady Day
and wont nothing like the bustling sounds of Basie

Louie and Pearl Bailey
to lay and waste a crazy day away.

back when lazy summer days
consisted of playing outside
and staying outside
till someone cried "Streetlight"
Dashing onto front porches
citronella torches and candles in cans
Fish Fry Fridays and fruit stands
Saturday Morning Cartoons
street leaf-boat races
happy faces and sandlots
sleep over's and pull out cots

back when all we got
was good enough
even if it wasn't brand new
when you finally got it
it was new to you
won't nothing wrong with a hand-me-down
it made you thankful for older cousins
you just became better
at playing the dozens

Man, how I miss those days
when play fights didn't get anyone hurt
and real fights determined your worth
when having the upper hand
meant you were willing to help the other man
cause down was just where we all began

Lazy Summer Afternoons

Spoken Soul

I'm a child of soul music... When rhythm and blues was more emotion than formula for air play. I came up listening to artists who pour their hearts out in their lyrics and who had bands that played true musicianship. When a song was actually composed. It had a verse, a chorus, a second verse, a vamp, a musical segway and in the really good songs there would be a spoken from the soul breakdown where the artist just poured out their whole heart and a ballad was born. I so miss the day when you could hear those soulful whalers on the radio singing those long so in love with you notes. What was a sample then? No one sampled music, you created it. You pulled from your experiences, your pleasures and your pains, your heartaches and hurts, your loves and losses and lessons of cost, and you added your creativity and soul to it, seasoned with the flavor of the area you lived in, and it was original.

I'm sick of this microwave music society of today. And I get that every generation has to be relevant and leave their contribution to the history of music, but this crap can't honestly be called a contribution. If I have to hear one more made up name, teenaged idiot, with no vocal ability perform their two lines and a hook looped in auto tune song on another awards show, I don't know what I'll do.

I know it's the industries fault. They're just exploiting the ignorance of today's youth in order to perpetuate a cycle of poverty and stupidity through cultural hypnosis, and the generations most affected have no clue that they're being brainwashed into perpetual ignorance. They believe they're actually trend setters. Ever since "Get Silly" it's only gotten stupid and more stupid. I truly fear that it will never turn around and three generations from now, music will be lost to them. Noise will be the new trend.

When caught in a downward spiral, pull up. How long are we going to allow ourselves to freefall before we begin to pull up? If it's true that what goes around comes around, then when will we see the likes of another Sam Cooke or Donny Hathaway? What cycle is this that's being repeated, because I can't in my forty years recall an era drenched in as much idiocy? Is this the new 70's? The rebirth of disco? Is this the new revolution? If so, I pray it stops being televised... Give me that old soul back. That soft spoken soul.

WOMAN

Her beauty has never impeded me. Intrigued with her femininity,
She has always moved me to pay attention.
To take notice... To focus on her worthiest attributes
When merely her eyes gave glance they caused mine to
Look deeper into her smile.
Given a second chance to take notice of her dimpled cheek
And to hear the melody in the voice with which she speaks
When her soft spoken hellos sang to me
And made my world move like a slow dance. No...
Her beauty has never been my hindrance.
At her entrance it was more than apparent that royalty graced the
room... When she faced the room her neck line drew more attention
than her breast line
And her hand was more revered than her behind, because She
carried herself magnificently...
She captivated intrinsically
Without explicitly parading her sexuality
And I was given audience, captivated by her mentality
And we spoke compatibly for hours upon end
And I welcome the pleasure of her presence again
In as much as a touch was ever felt
Only the touch of her hand was ever dealt
In our simple parting goodbye.

And my respect for her total being grew greater
Because she never tempted my eye.
Her beauty is the signature by which she signs her name.
My eyes have sought her autograph time and time again
And it's with reverence that I look upon her.

A Letter to My Younger Self

If I could write a letter to my younger self I would tell me:

At four years old, your first loss of a loved one will be hard, but remember all the good times. The things your Great Grandfather shared with you will stay with you all your life. He's the reason you like to get dressed. Spend more time with the elders in the family, they're part of the best education system to which you'll ever have free access. Blood is one thing, but Family is what's most important. All those who say they're your blood, won't be your family. The bad things that adults do aren't your fault. Sometimes bad things happen to good people. It's not God's fault either. Always remember to thank him for your protection. He has a special shield around you. Never go anywhere with Tommy by yourself... You can be friends with every girl in your kindergarten class at the same time, but they can't ALL be your girlfriend at the same time. They frown upon kissing in the second grade, but inside the big tire on the playground is a good hiding spot if she just has to kiss you. You'll only get caught once. As you get older, the prettiest girl in the school and the not so pretty girl in the school make great friends equally. It's not what's on the outside that matters. The little redhead girl in seventh grade will break your heart, but go ahead and like her anyway. Oh yeah, they're NOT going to let you name your baby brother Da'sucka. Some excuse about not wanting him picked on as a kid... If they'd only known it wouldn't be his name, but his mouth that got him into the most trouble and you into the most fights, they might would've reconsidered. But he turns out to be really cool and you love him more than anything. Try not to say "Stop touching me!" on the trip to Myrtle Beach. Daddy will never let you live it down. That... and getting lost at the State Fair will forever be your albatross. Okay... at fifteen years old two very significant things happen in your life. Both are you get a job. Now, I understand your logic and all; with it being your first time, that two condoms should be extra safe... but trust me on this... One is enough. And for some odd reason, having a 21yr old girlfriend at fifteen is NOT cool with Ma. She throws dirt in ya game on that one REAL hard. Pop...? It's all copasetic. The first girl to make your world move in slow motion, you'll date all through High School. Off and on for a couple years after... Pops gonna tell you to breakup with her around year two. "Relationships don't have to end on a bad note. It was good and now it's done." I didn't get it then. You'll get lots of opportunities to come to understand. Now, this is a bit tricky... As much as I'd love to tell you who and who not to, what, when and where to be... you go through some things that ultimately shape and make you me. A lot of it's due to mistakes and they cost you greatly. You're going to endure some pains that seem unbearable. Your heart will be broken progressively worse each time you choose to love, BUT don't let it hinder you from loving even harder the next time. It's worth it... The hurt that hardens you will heal and a daughter's love will restore you after some years. You were created for a purpose greater than you know... and the journey towards destiny is treacherous, but go you must, for thousands are depending on you. It'll take a while but you'll learn to draw strength from God. Listen to the Spirit within you. Your ear has been anointed to hear from him. I almost forgot... Friendship is based on how you treat a person, not how they treat you. You'll always be a true friend. Those who remain in your life throughout the years, you'll know are true friends to you. I'm looking forward to you having a great run at this life, Chet.

Good Luck,

P.S. You liking art, music, fashion, architecture and poetry more than cars and sports is going to pay off in such a major way it's ridiculous!!! Do ya thing, Mini Me!

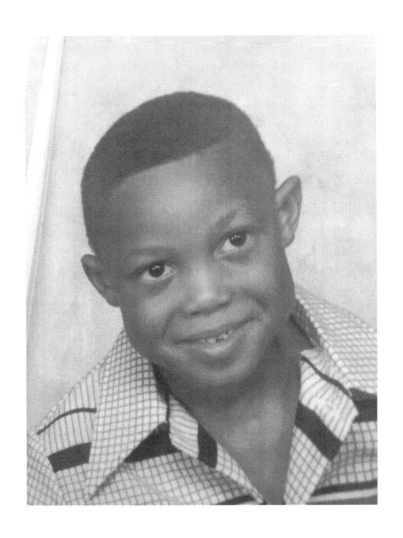

30/30 CHALLENGE PIECES

Heavy Palms

A Word Against the Hurting

In folded arms you choose to
Allow he bruise you.
Return to... where?... a crime is being committed.
30 seconds, and he did it again.
How many kisses does it take to ease your pain?
How many times will you believe the SAME lie...?
How many times... when YOU said, "I can't believe it"
Did you repeat it, to convince yourself HE didn't mean it?
Why let him keep using the SAME LINE?
In thy sane mind, while you defend...
30 seconds happened again.
How much time passed between rests?
You could hold your breath between this time and the last time
and the NEXT
But how long can you go without breathing?
How wrong is BLEEDING for "Love"?
He's misleading you, Love, if he's mistreating y' Love.
Every bruise she covered up was competing for love...
Battered bodies and broken hearts just pleading for love...
Never seeing an END
Never minding 30 seconds; he'll do it again.
What must I do... to redefine you?
Let me remind you...
Real MEN don't love with heavy palms or hardened fists.
Love might hurt, but not like this.

Let me love you in DEED... in WORD... in REAL...
In... Time your hurts will HEAL, but don't spend TIME letting it
KILL.
30 seconds... rest. 30 SECONDS... breath. 30 seconds till DEATH...
he'll do it again.
Get AWAY... tell someone... SAY something!
Don't let HIM hide behind shades over YOUR eyes...
Long sleeves in summer time...
Another made-up EXCUSE...
Don't be DECEIVED into ACCEPTING his ABUSE.
There is no reason good enough to believe in.
Don't let him treat you wrong.
Real men's hands are STRONG enough to hold you...
Enfold you in his arms...
And restrain from ever doing you any harm.

Stop domestic violence against women. We need our REAL MEN to
be Real friends and intervene on behalf of some of these women.
We need our women to stop accepting less than his best. The idea
that every 30 seconds a woman somewhere is being abused should
be enough to give you pause... If it's that many HE's hurting that
many HER's... odds are you know one.

BLACKEN AMERICA
A Homophones Challenge Piece

There would be wood where their noses grow
These Pinocchio's know no bounds.
Bound in paperback publications
Back when public Haitians weren't so criticized...
Before we realized their lies
Seeing through real eyes
What critics sized as a minute issue
Meant it was minute in their eyes
And therein lies the problem.
LIES...
For those who've told no tales
The bell tolls to tell
What needs to be exposed.
TRUTH in EXPO's...
Exhibitionism is inhibited by LIES inhabited
Make-believe incorporated...
High-end Corp. paraded mass deception
Like a marauders masquerade
Mask a raiding our finances they got master paid.
Master bated the line
We masticated the bait on the hook
And just like the Indian's
In the end
We got took.
Hoodwinked... Bamboozled... Lead astray... Run amuck...

The rich man got richer
The poor man got .... stuck!
Waiting on FEMA to send one bus to save all of us
Busting headlines as the levees burst
Then bursting out cursing as the waters worsened.
Where the hell's the water!? Not a drop to drink.
Drowned in the drink
Sinking and submersed in sewage
Sanitation's unthinkable for sanities sake.
The water's undrinkable and humanity breaks.
For a poor man there is no escape
And the waters kept pouring
Keeping the poor in.
Is it Justice or Just us?
Seen any neighbor hood's in your neighborhoods?
Or does neighbor hood watch really mean
Stalk and kill?
To be coal complexioned on a cold day
Complicated the matter.
But would it mattered had the shooter been black?
As a matter of fact...
Record... statistic or opinion...
How many accidental white kid's deaths have you heard mentioned
At the hand of a NON-white man?
NONE... (The E is silent)
Quietly pray not to awake the sleeping giant.

That we keep the dream
And not meet the violent with violence...
Cause that last shot
Rang out like the words of Gil Scott
"And the Revolution will NOT be Televised"
We can't tell if eyes be watching with ill intent
But we're sick of being watched
I bet the verdict tells what time it really is.
Don't watch your watch.
The clock on the wall's about to call
If Humpy don't fall
It was just another lynching.
LIES were the intention
Failed to mention he had over 200 Grand.
PAY ATTENTION!
In the Grand scheme of things
It's exactly what it seems.
It don't mean a thing...
It's just another NIGGA!

Discover N.A.P.P.Y.

Snap, crackle, pop...
Get in that kitchen
Them naps on your neck ain't nothing to play with.
Oooooh, you got Beady-beads...
You got hair like steel wool,
Girl, you Nappy-head...
And these were all the things we heard said as kids.
Irrevocable harm they did
To the image of what true beauty really is.
We failed to see the beauty
In her locks growing naturally.
We placed stock in the deception
Of others perceptions
And lost the value in the concept of
Black Is Beautiful.

Why would we do this to ourselves?
Delve with me just a little deeper
Let me speak unto the heart of the matter.
Cause the matter's not just your hair.
That's just the mask you've come to wear
To hide the face of your inner self-hate.

It's the concealer...
The confused foundation in which is lain
All the cover-ups of your true identity...

You call it Makeup
But wake up... it's make believe
Make believe I'm someone other than me...

It's eye shadow...
An illusion of a longer face
As opposed to a wider brow.
Like this befits your race somehow...

It's denying the prominence of your forehead...
That once proudly displayed our crowns.
But now we slay our nappy ROOTS
So they lay down
And cover our shame with bangs.
Afro centricity is pained.

Break the chains of disillusion's beauty.
Come back to who we truly used to be.
Profess it exponentially.
Be BOLD and BEAUTIFUL...
Restore the Glory in our H.I.S.tory.
Let your story speak of Kings and Queens
Their Royalty is seen
In the length of your neck and structure of your cheeks.
The flare of your nostrils speak
Of generations...

Of nations across seas and oceans
Where languages lost,
Let it be spoken by the symbolic token of your crown...
The celebration of your demonstration.
The acknowledgement of your past
The self-proclamation that you're FREE AT LAST
From the trickery of assimilation
Embrace our Holy Nation and Royal Priesthoods
Uncover your face and face the world as we should.
Happily N.A.P.P.Y.
Natural And Proud Proclaim Yourself.
Not Another Perm Presented Yearning to be somebody else.
Now A Purpose Personified YES!

YES! I'm Naturally Blessed...
With thick lips and wide hips
And curves that could sink ships
If water made waves as I'm contoured.
This gaze beneath my brow isn't imitated in eye liner
It's been passed down through generations of strong genes.
This sun kissed complexion is natural perfection.
It can't be duplicated by laying in some machine...
My shoulders are broader
My neck is longer...
My breast are fuller
My back is stronger...

And I birthed the entire earth,
So my stretch-marks are records of history.
And man beholds no other creation on earth as high as me.
I AM Black Gold...
MAMA AFRICA'S Brown Skin...
And I LOVE the N.A.P.P.Y. state of mind I'm in.

DIAMOND IN THE ROUGH

A Sonnet

From out of the darkness we came
Purposed in one frame of mind
Uniquely created the same
A masterpiece by design
Indelibly marked, "been kissed by the night"
Our souls pressed like coal
We sparkle like studded speckles of light
When out of the valley we rose
Through shadows of death, surrounded by evil
Awaiting the break of dawn
We proudly pressed, a united people
Determined to ever press on
Linked like chains by the shade of our skin
Our bond strengthened by the Spirit within

The Makings of a Man
An Ode

"Tie your shoes...
Tuck your shirt in...
Take your hands out your pockets, son.
Stand up straight
Did you wash your face?"
...
See, here is where the lesson's begun.

It wasn't by accident that lack was sent packing
Strong backs were bent sacking yields from cotton fields to bring back in
Stacking bales of tobacco
Hacking stalks and trees
And they did it all for these...
Stolen moments of
"Someday"
And most never visualized the dream
They only clung to the hope that one day they'd be seen
As a man.
Looked at with a modicum of respect
In place of the neglect that they'd been raised on
To be praised on by their women
Adored by their daughters
And made the mold from which their son's would become
This was the glint of hope to which they held
To overcome the ropes from which they hung.

"Always use your head, son.
Don't let your friends do your thinking...
Be a man of your word and tell the truth
Cause this is what real men do..."
...
So, I never lied to my father.
I clinched fists with the best of um
Tell the rest of um "I'm ready!
If they won't some... COME GIT SOME!"
He lookin at my Mama and ask me if I had a problem?
I answered, did he want one!
Cause I ain't NEVER scared
I bust heads and solve problems
"X" that out...
I ain't gotta deal with it again.
I ain't lookin over my shoulder
I already told ya "I'm READY!"
And I AIN'T EVER RAN FROM A MAN!

"Lord, why am I so angry?
Please don't let me kill anyone
My heart's healing, but my mind's become a time bomb
Just one more tick and I'm done...
I no longer long to be what I've become
Lord, I need you to take this rage away
Recede these rainy days
And let sun rays wash away these pains

Teach me how to forgive
Cause if not...
I might not live
And I don't want to die in this cage.
Please let Peace release me."

"Your steps are ordered, son.
There's a calling on your life...
In all things...
Acknowledge Christ
And He will direct your path."
...
At last.

I've traveled a million miles to find this land
Crossed oceans, seas and desert sands
All to stand rooted in this place
I faced enemies I couldn't see
I war continually
I knew eventually I'd reach my journey's end.
It's been a long time coming...
Overcoming hurdles kept me running
But the pace for this race need not be swift
Nor need I be strong...
Cause I've not made it here on my own
I've only endured unto the end.
...
And these are the makings of a man.

FOR COLORED MEN

And this is for colored men whose hearts have only been filled with dreams, ambitions and good intentions... shattered by the gathered discontent of black women for pretentious reasons... Battered by she's dissatisfied, because she fantasizes these soap opera lives and won't give to live within her means. Stretching him check to check but the in-betweens won't let him forget... how hard it is in this real world for black guys trying to create their own opportunity. And you have the nerve to look at me with eyes that look right through me... Like I'm less than the man I know I am... Like you couldn't give a damn... or you could care less about my being a success. So, I confess... I detest the way you look at me sometimes. But "She"... She has supportive eyes. So, when you think you need a reason why; I need a reason to. I need a refuge... and what you refuse, I know she's willing to do. She doesn't fight me to try to right me, but corrects me when I'm wrong with strong embraces... Rather than gettin' all up in Brothers faces with loud-talking, head-shaking attitudes... being insistently rude to prove my equal, then choosing to be intentionally dismissive in the bedroom... She's consistently submissive... purposefully attentive... doesn't mind bringing a Brother a glass of tea, or simply giving him the little respect he needs... like saying "Baby, could you please", rather than "Nigga, why don't you"... This is for colored men. You women ain't gonna like it, but I'm gonna write it... cause my name isn't Tyler Perry... This ain't fairytales and make believe. But "She"... She caters to my needs in as much as a feeling is felt... we become confident in self, because she tells me what I'm worth to her... Everything... What this woman brings to a man, black women don't seem to understand... and you wonder why we marry white women. Because we don't wanna fight women... There can only be one man, and you think you can wear the pants better than I can... So, the end... She wins. And this is for colored men...

This is for colored men who've been beaten, battered and broken by the weight of silent burdens in their lives who continue to press on... And this is for colored men... Black backs bended and bunched over... 30min lunch over... but mandatory overtime, cause bills don't get paid on part time. And you can't afford to call, so be here tomorrow or not at all... Peter won't get paid today; Paul took it all... And I can't take the strain that's going on inside my brain... I'm a KING in CHAINS! Shackled to middle-class poverty. Only one check away from living in the streets! But it's an honest living??? How can I honestly feel alive when all I can do is barely survive? I remember once upon a time when I hustled... I made a killing. But God's willing me to be Writeous... that I might just right my wrongs. So, in Him... through my trials, I press on. And this cage I'm in is shrinking... This rage I'm in is swelling... and these chains can no longer restrain me! This cage can't contain me! I'm ANGRY... to the sound of genocide. I'm angry to a nation of taken lives... A nation mistaken of taking eyes off of prize... A fallen land. So, I'm calling every fallen man to take a stand against the wiles of the enemy. Let not your fall be your defeat. Be not retreated... Roll call will not be repeated. SOUND OFF like a WARRIOR for GOD if you BELIEVE it! THIS IS WARFARE!!! IT DONT GET NO MORE FAIR!!! And the REVOLUTION will NOT be televised...

This is for colored men whose heavy laden hearts have been mistaken, taken for granted and misunderstood... This is for men whose wives were no good... For those souls who've told no tales, yet whose lives do lies seem to know well, for the sake of despising liars... "Hate on me haters"... and them "Baby making see ya laters"... cause "It's hard to keep a good man (unless you make a baby) minded mother's"... Can't wait to get a brother under covers... for that 18 yearlong commitment. Notice, I didn't say relation; cause all she really wanted was compensation. And now he wonders where Daddy went... Across the nation support is sent, but not given cause he's made to resent being a father for the sake of a dollar. Call it restitution governed by an institution that could care less about the solution to broken families... Just another demand of me to force the threat of penitentiary... Life without the possibility of parole. So they sentence you to Ex-wife without the possibility of control... Baby-Mama drama gets old after a few years... Now dealing with resentment and tears for absence sake... Wherein lies the mistake of believing she could keep him by having kids. And this is for colored men... This is for colored men who've been lost to confusion... under the illusion that seclusion is the solution. For the lonely that can only find solace in another man... The "Homo-Down-Low-Undercover-Brother" Man? Confusing homosexual for homosapien. "I'm not Gay... I'm just a man who likes to sleep with other men"...???... Gay man is an oxymoron! Was Sodom and Gomorrah make believe!? Created Adam, but then He gave him Eve... two men cannot conceive, but its accepted everyday by society. I used to like variety... but I could NEVER understand how you could ever love a woman but want a man. This is for colored men betrayed, abused, abandoned, confused... raised in the admonition of women... criticized, scrutinized, ashamed... who believe it's too late to change... who've lost their identity to their sin. Whatever place you're in... God is a healer and deliverer. You don't have to stay in bondage to sin. And this is for colored men...

GUILTY

I'm guilty
Guilty of not painting her unique
But with broad strokes of the same brush
A brush I've used to paint so many
Who looked like her.
Cornered in her circumstance
Hands tied behind her back
For lack of a better opportunity
I painted her beneath me...
Loud and outspoken
Eloquently challenge
Unversed to converse
More likely to "conversate"
I painted her ghetto...
Single mother
Five children, four fathers
Her Constitution reads
Equally entitled to
Housing, food stamps
And the pursuit of child support
I painted her trifling
Negligible
Insignificant
And typical
I painted her with malice
Disdain and embarrassment

I painted her with
Lack of self-respect
Her disheveled appearance
Was something I'd rather forget
Displeasing to me
A visual offense
And I painted it with
"Why would she come out looking like that?"
I'm guilty of not painting her
Caring and considerate
Giving of her time
Because that's all she could afford to give.
I'm guilty of not painting her
Loving and kind
But humbled at the time
Because that's the only way she can afford to live
I'm guilty of not painting her
Once raped, twice widowed and divorced
With two husbands having served on the force
I'm guilty of not painting her
With strength and courage
Perseverance and determination
I'm guilty of not painting her
Desperation at times

Her despondency
Or despair
I quickly painted her with
"I really don't care"
And I'm guilty
Of never knowing her story

HEAVY WEIGHS THE CROWN

President Barack Obama
They said it could never be done
I did it
In the face of opposition
I never remitted
Never requited
Never relinquished the dream
To accomplish the things
That had never been seen
But heavy weighs the crown of the king
These shoulders hold a whole world upon them
When fears of conspiracy rears
I stand among them
Fearlessly
When shadows of darkness come
I run towards what they run from
And heavy weighs the crown
No shield
No armor found
Just a sword and the heart of a warrior
And heavy weighs the crown.

AN EVERYDAY EXISTENCE
A Workshop Challenge Piece

I slept through the night
Snoring yet peacefully
Yawning breath at dawning light I see
My eyes wake to a new day
And God exists

Water runs
Toilet
Toothpaste then tub
Kitchen lights
Morning tea warming up
And bills exist

Traffic's moving
Much slower than I would be
The scent of fumes at packed intersections
Impede me
Merging lanes and alternating signals
Would please me
Light rails and skyways if need be
Wishing I could fly
Time passing by less easily
And frustrations exist

Keyrings and locked doors
File cabinets and desk drawers
Restroom stalls and tiled floors
Carpet
Computers
Keystrokes and Post-It notes
Cubicles and conference calls
Motivational posters hung on every wall
And work exists

Paper and pen
Pencils and paintbrushes
Pandora and a passion for the poetic
Pursuing purpose
Presenting possibility
Power of persuasion and probability
And I exist...

THIRST

Water for Africa
If waterfalls of tears
Could create an oasis
With each drop
I'd cry for year's non stop
My eyes
Would spill rivers
For heartlands
Of dry sands
I'd cry
Monsoons
To erase the traces
Of desert places
If I were rain
I would fall
Again
And again
Everyday
To wash your pain
Away

Victim of a Siren's Song

Inspired by Karol Bak's painting Alter Ego

If poetry teaches us one thing
Of this one thing be sure
In this life where no thing is fair
All is fair in love and war.

Sullen...
Sunken...
Sinking my beating heart
Like ships lost to a Siren's song
She sings softly to my soul
She sings sorrowful ballads of woe
The most beautiful hurt
A heart could ever know
She sings of love lost long ago
She sings poetically to my soul
Words with wings like flying things
See sings and her melodies intrigue me
She serenades me in her tears
Her loss echoing through her fears
Till I sleep upon her oceans floor
Shipwrecked and abandoned
Heartbroken and alone
Her traitorous grave now becomes my home
Another sailor lost at see
Lost sight the night she called to me

Singing from her rocks of heartaches past
From where breakers brake
And loves like breaking waves crash
Dashing like raging rapids thrashing
Bashing aimlessly against her cliffs
Her treacherous ways
Loves traitorous heart she breaks
In oceans of tears lovers drift away
Ever downwards...
Toward sea bottoms and ocean floors
Only to dream her song forever more
Enslaved to a Siren's song.

MESSAGE IN A BOTTLE

I Write
Like my life depended on it
Cause I need it
And some of you just want it.

I need it like I need air to breathe.
I bleed indigo and ebony
Till the pages of My Unsung Soul are black and blue
And my heart pours beautiful pains...

So heavy are the rains
That each tear drop bruises my cheek.
I cry rivers of ink
And just when I think I'm through
I reminisce of you
I'm overwhelmed and this well never runs dry.

Try as I might
I spent the day counting a thousand nights
Where dreams left me breathless
Where all I had left was this...
So I poured out my heart like an abyss
A bottomless ocean of emotion
From which each line riffs like waves
And sorrows drift upon them like notes in bottles
In hopes of your finding my tomorrows...
I paint these poetic sunrises.

Dance with Me in the Moonlight

A pale moonlight and the mood is right
Its thirteen minutes till midnight.
Come meet me in the middle of this crossroads
Lost souls wander there
But I just like to wade and ponder where
The wayward wander aimlessly
Some unashamedly call it yonder
But for me it's a place of retreat.
Walk with me under the stars
These neon lights to life shine bright
Exes and dollar signs light up the night
Take a flight with me into ecstasy
Let's see how Destiny really feels
Leave the Matrix... Just swallow the red pill
And come dance with me.
Make plans with me and take my hand
Let me lead you through this no-man's land
Please you to houses of ill repute
Your reputation precedes you
I'm pleased to... make your acquaintance
Now, might only I acquire a kiss...?
Let us break Judas wheat for lover's bread
And sup raspberry wine as fed

To commemorate this traitorous moment...
In remembrance of me, do this...
Sin... and betray with a kiss
Forever Yours ...

The Devil

PONDERING POETIC

I have a propensity for pondering that perplexes the common senses, since common sense isn't all that common, simply speaking, I prefer to think in the poetic, underline the subliminal, highlight the spiritual, white-out the mistakes and write out the takes in life. I let my re-thinks speak twice and you can call it a retake. My life needed a remake for each mistake I made, so re-righted my wrongs in red ink He paid and called it take two. On second thought, let me take a second to think a minute... how many second chances can one be given? How many takes and re-takes to right-out the mistakes and wrongs? How many chances to write out the songs of unsung sorrows and regrets? How many yesterdays will tomorrow forget for me to only live in these stolen moments? Pondering consequences, flashbacks and glimpses of non-sequential incidences play in my brain. So I'm now sporadically ashamed, but you can't see that pain from my outside. Only the panoramas of my mind display that misery clearly; to the point that these ponderings leave me weary and again I'm back to thinking about second chances. Glances into my past. How many chances have you had since the last time you said "this is the last time"? Ponder on it for a moment... I'll take a minute to wait a second.

I speak in ink and I think in the poetic.

DESTINATIONS UNKNOWN
A Series Piece

Even though the sign on the corner boasted DEAD END as a proclamation for me not to tread in... I like walking down dead end streets. There may be something to see. And it's not curiosity getting the best of me, I just know better than most that opportunity doesn't stop simply because the road does. Because what was there before the road was... is still there lingering in the distance. It just take a little persistence to continue. So, I commend you who can see an open road but dead ends don't offend you and you welcome destinations unknown.

Like place holders these lots lay vacant. Like empty seats in movie theaters where you can never find two together... Like weather beaten trees where some branches bear no leaves and all you can see are the bare spots. I dare you stop to take a closer look... Like missing pages of a book the story often unfolds between the lines, and you're missing the second chapter but judging me after the third, when you can't even begin to comprehend this broken word, because metaphorically speaking I'm an allegorical oracle, historically Beasting this spoken word. Unequivocally truth speaking I travel to desolated places, because the desolated embrace the truth with grateful faces. Though we be broken it takes an emboldened word to say something we haven't already heard.

I know I'm broken... Tell me how to be whole again. What I can behold in them is a desire to be seen for something other than sin.

Can you see me in compassion despite my fallen actions? Can you save a place for me at the table? If I were able I wouldn't need any assistance, but rather than embrace me you met me with resistance when I reached out... not looking for a hand-out, just a hand up so I could stand up; but you rather drop some change in my cup than look me in the eye and ask my name. But I know that all seasons change... and my destination remains unknown.

Mr. Bojangles

Yeah, you be that Chris Rock in Vanity Fair, I don't care where I came from; I'm just glad I'm not there, type of nigga. That token FRIEND laughing, joking, hoping to fit in and now you can't even smile the same... You gone change the game on 'um... You'll probably even change your name on 'um. Masquerades were made for hiding faces. I bet they wonder what your race is. Maybe they think it's a skin condition? Your blackness must be in remission or maybe you're just Blackish enough not to pay attention to what everyone else seems to know. The show must go on. Let's turn that frown upside down... Nothing's sadder than the tears of a clown and you've been Barnum and Bailey's for years... thinking you've been adopted by your peers, but one day they'll discover your deepest fears and then you'll be "that Nigger".

They'll feel utterly disrespected that you went all these years undetected. Really! (I just made air quotation marks, but you couldn't see it)... They called you Black, but you couldn't be it. As a matter of fact you turned your back to try to flee it, you just better hope you never need it. So, you wrote your own HiStory... a mystery, the lies you had to tell for those who never knew you to know you well. Prancing Mr. Bojangles... Pretending to be Mr. Tibbs, but your lack of identity leaves your dignity drib. It must be lonely. I can only imagine... denying myself the satisfaction of being who I AM, being who I was created to be... I couldn't begin to pretend not to be me.

But you make it seem so effortless... tell me how this could be. You seem to be a whiz of a wiz, if ever a wiz there was. If ever, oh ever a wiz there was you seem to be one because, because, because, because, because, because.......................... I can't even think of a reason.

So, we're off to see him; the wonderful wizard of Who? How's it feel to have become the spectacle of you? Does it hurt to pull back the curtains that you hide behind... wishing we all were blind to your charade? There's no pride in your parade, but you're the Grandest Marshal shame has ever made.

You can't comprehend how they see you. Ask any of them if they'd like to be you and no one would take your place, because the color of your skin won't erase... and there's not enough white out to write out your race. You'll always be a Black man... and they'll ALWAYS see a BLACK man. Your white maybes won't let you see a Black CAN. Mister prancin' dancin' Mr. Bojangles.

SAND DUNES OF SOLITUDE

Times ticking
Tocking to taking today away
Trying to tell tomorrow to stay away
Can't stop the sands of time
So I set sail to seven seas
To sever these
Sand dunes of solitary memories
Deserted in my mind
Mere moments that misery left behind
Memoirs of a misguided man
Couldn't compass my compassion
Found fault but never in the mirror
Reflections in retrospect are much clearer
But burnt bridges boast bad behaviors
Barricaded by barren sands
I would beg to barter to bear your care again
The time-lapse topography of desert lands
Show a shifting in the shaping of the sands
Should I be wishing for a sifting?
Searching where buried treasures stand
In sand dunes of solitary memories

Like a River

Like a river, run to me
Float comfortably upon the drifts of my shallows
Wade in me playfully,
Like Childs play in kiddy pools
Bare feet in brooks of cool
And glistening streams
When listening seems endearing
Lay back and place your ear in just below the surface
Hear the very purpose of your being
Repeating in every heartbeat
You can be fetal in me
Rebirth your worth and be free
Like flowing cascades of waterfalls
A reminiscent mist in the distance
A rushing come forth persistence
Spills in blue lagoons of my soul
As I come to know you show me more
Let me bask upon the beaches of your shore
Your reaches explore the depths of my being
Forever foreseeing destiny
Take me away till nothing's left of me
To be raptured would be heavenly
Angelically caught up in feathered ecstasy
Lift me away in angel's wings
Until new dawn's, new days bring
Let's run away like rivers

Up Against the Wind

Inspired by Christopher Young's entitled song
Pushing against the wind seems to be a theme for me
More time than less, struggle I see
Those unseen forces confronting my choices
Holding me captive inexplicably
It's despicably me... again
Made to choose a fate for glooms sake
Because this wind carried me the wrong way
Seeking protection against the wall
Fearing the stumbling and the fall
These walls are crumbling in on me...

Day after day press
No changes... no rest
Since birth it's been this way it seems
Night offers me the moon but clouds take it away
There are no stars left in my dreams
The swells of my soul never see high tides
I break constantly...

The shores of my heart are only salty
Their waters faultily retreated
And so, my pains repeated
Too many don'ts to want for anything
More than what yesterday's bring
Bitter memories of opportunities passed
Why is the question I ever ask

But why is a question I have no answer to
In another life I could have been you
But the breeze will be the breeze
And fallen leaves blow
With no question as to where
How fallen should I be to care
What tomorrow brings?

FADED PICTURES

Alzheimer's and Dementia

Passed the place of gracefully, these days hastily seem to be far less amazing. These memories seem to be fading and I feel a fog rolling in. These eyes aren't what they used to be. They seem not to recognize the things they used to see and familiar faces often feel new to me. I gaze into the distance hoping to see it clearly, but the visions I envision aren't nearly as vivid as I imagine. Thought it's good to see old friends again, it's more often than not that they're not there. I've gotten used to being corrected. It's so easy to be disrespected when you see things that just aren't there. I don't know why I like to go by the window and stare at sidewalks... or why most of the times spinning in my mind are me and numbers having quiet talks and it only makes sense to me. "Six one seventeen, six one eighteen, six one nineteen, six one twenty!" Why doesn't this make sense to anyone else but me...? They each have a place; I'm just trying to figure out where that place should be. "Six one seventeen, six one eighteen, six one nineteen, six one twenty! Six one fifteen, six one seventeen, six one eighteen, six one twenty!"

Repetition is the key. Somebody keeps moving my hands but that somebody isn't me, because I seem to have misplaced some things. I've been driving all of my life, but someone has taken my keys and they keep opening car doors to back seats... and I'm not sure anymore where we're going. But I'm becoming more comforted with not knowing what day this is or what name is his... If this is a game, I couldn't explain the rules to what game this is. All I know is that she leads me to the places I need be. She sees me... she feeds me... she makes following her easy and she's there every time I call her name. If getting old is a game, I must be winning; because this is the eightieth inning and I'm on deck for greater places.

Amazing Grace is dear to me. It's clear to see that I'm kept in family prayers and safe in the arms of a Savior who cares. So, my cares can waste away from day to day, and though my pictures fade, in my mind I can still see the parade of all the faces I've ever known, all the places I've ever gone and all the harvests of all the seeds I've ever sown... It makes this a bit easier, though burdensome I still feel at times... but I never see it when I look into their eyes. They only show me love, respect and dignity.

TRANSCENDENTAL LOVE

Not for the sake
Of having something to say
But
For the love of poetry
Words play
Like kindergarten recess
In the recesses of my mind
Unveiling metaphors in rhyme
Ever since that first line
That first time
I wrote a love letter
In seventh grade
And it made
Seven girlfriends
That's when I fell in love with the pen...
She became my closest friend
We started going steady in high school
Her free verse had me break all the rules
We used to write Haiku's
Like kisses in the hall between classes
And we made passes at poetic overtures
Until ballads became passé
We could pass the day away
In iambic pentameter
We had no boundaries or parameters
On what we could say

Uncommonly an anomaly
Our vernacular was spectacular
We'd peruse the rings of Saturn in Simile
Drifting like snow in December... We

Transcended time and place
Became out of space
When the lines
Were too much for the page
Now engaged
We spoken word
And you never heard love like ours
We parley knee deep into the wee
Hours of early morning
Aint nothing like that A.M. between the sheets
I gently journal her in fresh ink
Until...
Poetic perfection

SICK AND TIRED

I'm sick and tired...
I'm sick and tired of band wagoner's.
Protagonists posing as black activists
Waving black flags and raising black fists
In protest against a system
You perpetuate,
When so called black love
Is just hate demonstrated with bias.
Your pious actions of dissatisfaction
Are just an excuse to rage at the abuse
Of those you never knew.
When the truth is it's you who kill your own...
Where's the rage over your local news
When two of your homeboys
Killed two other dudes
Because of an argument
Over a pair of shoes
A bag of weed
And some side chick?
Why don't THAT make you sick?
I'm left to wonder why
When silence is kept and all I hear is crickets...
But you steadily punching tickets for the big fight
Promoting the HYPE of REVOLUTION
But you only moving through revolving doors.
And revolution has more than one meaning...

I'm sick and tired of brothers leaning on crutches
With their same ole such and such's
As eloquently expressed in Kim Field's "How Come"
When you gon' find a different outcome?
How long you gon' shout dumb excuses?
When you gon' learn to put your words to better uses?
Oh, I'm sick and tired...
I'm sick and tired of riot after riot
As an excuse to loot Walmart's and Dollar stores
But you won't make your dollar do more
Because every black Friday
You at Walmart filling carts
And posting vides on WorldstarHIPHOP
But you won't shop black businesses
And keep black dollars in black communities
You won't support entrepreneurs or opportunities
But you're constantly shouting unity chants
Like Black Lives Matter...
No Justice No Peace...
Like you gon' see it
And I'm constantly wondering when you gon' be it?
Cause then we might prevail as a people...
I'm sick and tired of seeing equal rights
Treated like sequel fights on Showtime...
We already boycotted the bus line
Not to ride in the back seat one time

Why we gotta do it again!?
Oh, we back to the meaning of revolution...
This is the remedial class of ... The Evolution of Self Worth
When we gon' stop dealing self-hurt,
Seek self-help and start healing ourselves?
When we gon' stop waiting on someone else?
Did I say I was sick and tired?
I'm sick and tired of girl's twerking
And guys shirking responsibility instead of working
Sick of you claiming they're jerking you around
But you stepped to the interview dressed like a clown.
I'm sick of those sagging' dragging as
Like no class degenerates

I'm sick of seeing belligerent behavior
Advocated on social media...
I'm sick of Wikipedia
I'm sick of music that doesn't make sense
I'm sick of excusing ignorance for innocence
I'm sick of duck face selfies
I'm sick of Snapchat and Instagram
I'm sick of seeing people with their face in a phone cam
Like it's the meaning to life!
I'm sick and tired
And sick and tired
And sick and tired

And sick and tired
And sick and tired
Of being SICK and TIRED of
Seeing sick and tired people
Not give a damn...
Why aren't you as sick and tired as I am?

GOTTA JONES

Inspired by D'Angelo's "Jonz In My Bonz"
Me and this jones go way back
Like lay back seats, futons and recliner chairs
We been kickin it for years
But I ain't ever been able to kick it
I just stick it to the side from time to time
But it stays stuck in my mind
And we come reminiscent like Elmer's Glue
And construction paper
This jones is a labor of love
I carry her everywhere... wanting to roll'er
Wishing I could afford a stroller
Must be what I weighed on Mama's hip
Tuggin on my shirttail every trip
Yellin "I want I want I won't"
And it would be all good except I don't
I don't wanna give in to a jones named Skin
She would be the death of me
Temptation to Sin...
I've come too far
Got too much to lose
But she's like the Neo-Soul to my Rhythm & Blues
And I love to listen to her
Like that sexy neighbor you choose never to meet
Cause you know it'll be on from the moment you speak
And I ain't never been one to bite my tongue
So I gotta jones...

HARD KNOCKS LIFE

2:22a.m.

I sit here in silence pining for words to say to you... Words that might someday resonate with you. I'm asking God for a breakthrough, that you might hear me clearly... cause I believe you've truly lost the ability. And the cost has yet to reveal itself in your eyes. It'll be too late when you finally realize. So, I'm sitting here. Time traveling in my mind to a future you've already left behind. Seeing what you could have been... should've would've been had you only kept your mind off Bulls#it. Oh, my bad... was I supposed to say sin? I been out the box. They can't fit me back in. So, here it is...

Babygirl, this world comes atcha hard

It's cold and careless; leaves you marked and scarred

For life

When in an instant, your choice ain't right

Walk wit me...

Come and talk wit me

This pimp game tight

I been spittin this ish for all yo life

Ain't nothing new in the game

The world revolves, but remains the same

And what goes around... comes around

These lil niggas just pickin up what I been put down

And you let it gotcha open

Should've never let it gotcha to start

He just played yo as' over yo heart

Cause you can't listen wit ya legs spread

Thought I taughtcha to use your head
But yall lil chicks fall for every line being said
"Lend me your ear... Let me whisper secrets to your sacred places"
I used to love to see the look on their faces
Hook, line and sinker... She'd linger on every word I said
To git between her legs I played wit her head
Now you gone fall for the same game
I told ya
The world don't change
And that nucca ain't even worth his own name
You ain't gotta listen to me
But you gone learn today
Cause life gone teach you the hard way
I hate to see it happen
But maybe it's for your own good
Ghetto minds stay stuck in the hood
When you look around
Ten years...
And see you're still right there
Maybe then you'll begin to care
Whatcha Mama tried to teach ya
Daddy tried to reach ya
But you let your foolish heart mislead ya
Threw ya whole life away for puppy love
And didn't even know the real meaning of
At seventeen your life ain't even begun

It's been all fun and games till now
Step yo as' into the REAL World
I hope it smack the taste outcha mouth!
Cause you gone find out what real life is about
This world don't move for lil chicks with attitudes
The lil game you playing ended yesterday
You wanna play grown
But GROWN DON'T PLAY!
Now you gone pay
For the rest of yo life
So gone and gitcha lil Wendy's money right
I hope Wendy's got a retirement plan
Cause you failed to understand
You just burst the bubble you been living in
Welcome to consequence
Trouble and hard times will find ya
Life has a funny way to remind ya
Of the little mistakes you made that cost the most
When you hear it whisper
Listen up close
You'll hear the devil laughing atcha
He didn't even have to catch ya
You wanted to mess around on his playground
Wanted to lay down
You found your way down
I pray to God you just don't stay down

Cause spiral staircases to the bottom
Take the same way back up
You think you're ready for this journey
I wish you luck.
Live ya life
I can't give nothing else but advice
But it won't do no good if you don't take it
Hope I'm around to see you make it
But you stole my heart, just to break it
Cause you gone answer for every mistake
I leave you in God's amazing grace
I hope you find your right place in life
Before I go... I'ma give ya one last piece of advice
When ya find yourself going left
And you can't find Right
Turn around and return to Christ
Remember I always love you
But I can't Save your Life
You gotta get your own walk right

Love Always,
Daddy

VOUS SEMBLEZ FAMILIERS

Got that feeling again...
That for old time's sakes feeling.
That... Let's go back down memory lane
Traveling feeling
That feeling
Like a love affair.

Got that stuck in my mind
Lost sense of time
Can't seem to find my way clear
Feeling.
That drunken haze
Love craze lazy days feeling
Visions of bedframes and ceilings
Dance in my head.

Spinning...
Like the rooms moving.
Losing all I've gained in choosing you.
Rendezvous' and secret places
This tryst of hidden faces
Never tells
Places we know all too well
And it seems
We haven't been here in a while...

I'll...
Try to refrain myself
Contain myself if nothing else
Slow the time
Racing out of control inside my mind.
Inner visions of surreally...

Reality reminiscent
Life's but a dream
But this dream isn't...

Indicative of a distant love
Lost in dream
Awaken hours seem
Only...
To keep me away
I sleep to meet another day
And maybe
This time
You'll...
Tell me your name.

BROTHER

They call me Brother
No other
title have I gone by
nor have I known why
title was needed to own
Un I dentified I
fit no description
their depiction of I is not my own
Why box me?
I find it hard to breathe
encase me in case I dare be free
Care be free to release me
Share I utter a spoken word
to ignite the fright
with every syllable heard
I burn fears and fan the flames
I need no title
I'm known by many names
But they call me Brother
Others of I come from one
A chosen nation
For my Father has many sons
I and I
we all Called
and marked for warriors death
we wage war till no more be left
Victorious for the Kingdom

ONLY POETS SAY MELANCHOLY

DISTANCE

A Father's Pain

It's been a long time since I put pen to line,
But my minds been pacing back and forth.
My rhymes been racing back and forth...
Like eyes following the lines of this text,
Somehow vexed, I recite my highs and lows.
My peaks and valleys speak of steeples and alleys.
Both, church bells and fare wells read in my memoirs.
I didn't mean to leave scars...
In some places that they are,
But it's too late to apologize.
I recognize this hardened place...
The look in my eyes is scarred my face...
Mistakes along the way
Cost me more than I thought I should have had to pay.
But every war is fair...
Every lesson learned from there... is paid for in gains of pain.
Shed tears for my Daughter
Water collected like pails of rain...
La Trails run down my face.
Couldn't Kindle the flame for the sake of my goodbye...
How many pails till my eyes run dry?
Fare thee well...
Is not my salutation, it's my prayer
For those I care, but have lost at see...
My inner visions, but they don't see me.

My Always

Minister, Mother
Daughter Sister Friend...
Wife, Companion, Aunt and Confidant.
With so great a care she fulfilled every role
No greater heart or more beautiful a soul
Than Lenora Freeman Speller we'll ever know.
Heaven holds her in high esteem...
Now living out her destiny and dream...
Of dancing before the King of Kings.
She is an instrument of Praise...
Dance is her weapon of warfare.
But where she is, there's no more war there...
Exalted high above the earth
So great her reward befits her worth.
She was more to many than most to some...
Spoke Grace, Peace and Life to everyone...
Love glowed from her locks to the tips of her toes
Flowed like flags, ribbons and white linens...
And rose like her Praise ascended on angel's wings.
When I think of her, I think of these things...
Hopefully forever and always I'll continue to war in Praise with my
Minister, Mother
Daughter Sister Friend...
Wife, Companion, Aunt and Confidant.
The name Lenora Freeman Speller will live forever...
Carried on winds and waves from Carolina to Kenya

Ascended on Praise that she'll never let us forget...
Poured out in tears like oil from Alabaster boxes...
And Called in Heaven as a song unto the Lord.
Well done, Minister Lenora...
Grace, Peace and Life be unto you.
My Sister and Friend

Loss: A Poet Extraordinaire Haiku

In memory of Keenan M. Gorham

My Soul yet so weeps
For an angel given wings.
Too soon gone it seems.

TILL WE MEET AGAIN

Till We Meet Again
I know sorrow's but for a moment
Though it seems this pain is haunting me.
I keep looking for the moment to pass
To find the joy inside our memories
But sorrow's hand is heavy.
He presses my chest
Till it pains me to breathe.
And my sides ache
For my breaking heart's sake
And this hollow in my soul seems endless.
Mourning for the morning.
Longing for the dawn to yet return
My darkest hour came
When loss of you I learned.
And still my heart is yearning
For reminiscent days and breaking light
Memories or moments we laughed into the night.
Shall ever we laugh again my friend?
Though it seems distant
Heaven is not that far away.
And it'll seem but as an instant
When we speak face to face.
I feel sorrow breaking now.
The aching in my chest has given rest
And these tears that stream

Now seem to comfort me.
They weep away a sweet release
And in sorrow's departing
Comes Peace.
Though my morrows are uncertain
And curtains of rain may pour again
The storms only last
Until they end
And it never rains forever.
Every weather has its reason.
For everything there's a time and a season.
A time to live... and a time to die
A time to laugh... and a time to cry
A time to meet... and a time to say good-bye.
Have rest in Peace.
Until again we meet
Whisper secrets on the wind to me from Heaven.

Sorrow's But for a Moment

These tears comfort me.
Weep away a sweet release.
Peace is soon to come.

Déjà vu

I would walk you through
weathered storms and trying times
Sing bitter sweet melodies and memories of past lives
Tell you tomorrows would-to-be's
If only these lines could relieve
Or ease the troubles you'll go through.
Daddy's little girl... mad at the world
Wishing for womanhood... Misunderstood
Love struck and stuck on stupid for cupid
Just smarter than a fifth grader
Harder than chocolate covered peanuts
But melted like M&M's in him&him hands
A sticky mess... you're stuck in
Measuring moments on a timeline of eternity
Wish you could only see what I see
I've been through your future
Stood atop the peaks you've yet to reach
I see so much further than you
But I can't live the life you choose
So I hope you choose wisely
Cause you remind me of a girl that I once knew

LIKE FEATHERS ON THE WIND

From behind my eyes
The view is like peeking through tear soaked lashed.
The lights are just as bright, but the silhouettes' are blurred.
Not so clear the lines that define the word... me.
Identity... is what I've chosen to be
And who I am,
Seed of another,
Son of a mother, who's seed of an unknown,
Speaks not pleasingly to my soul...
But reminds me daily in silence
The secrets we never speak.
The fruit of those who've chosen me...
And those I've chosen.
Love is thicker than blood...
But transfused ice water courses through my veins
For my blood's sake.
Blood forsaken
I was taken in by love,
Raised and praised by love
Made stronger so many different ways by love,
But that ice water still courses in my veins...
It pains me cold hearted
Like departed souls from warm bodies
Morbid corpses lay in my wake.
Take not of my hand and turn away...
For you'll only forsake me once.

There'll be no second chance
To again take of my hand...
Burn me in Spring...
When Summer fun is done you'll Fall
And need me to cross rivers of thin ice come Winter.
But then, you'll swim in these veins
Frozen soul's hold no forgiveness...
So, thy live and let live less
Will forever be the cry of my ashes.
Look not for me when I'm blown away.
Like Feathers on the wind
You'll never gather all together again.
We're strewn in too many different places.

Tears

My teary eyed... wipe thy weary eyes
And understand that, here, a grown man cries...
Longing to be with you
My aching heart is breaking too
Not a day's gone by
I haven't thought of you.
Looking back now in regret
Wishing I'd never left...
Vowing to love forever
That I might never forget
This pain of having loss.
This strain of having cost...
This shame of having caused
A single tear to fall
From the eyes of someone I love.
Need I apologize a million times?
I've shed a billion tears...
Wishing I could turn back the years,
But forgive my hands for being tied.
A thousand deaths I've died
And I'll likely die another hundred times,
But I'll count them not for sorrow...
For one of these tomorrow's I'll be home.
From afar I'll admire how you've grown.
And if by chance someday you'll give
Our love another chance to live

Ours tears be not in vain...
Our broken hearts will heal...
And you will be more to me
Than just one feature.
My teary eyed... set weariness aside
There's a wholeness where we let love abide.

HOPE FOR TOMORROW

Cello notes reverberating in my hollowed soul echo like songs of blue whales and tales of distant love. Persistent love calls of sorrow for morrows mourning and tomorrow morning I'll still long to see your face. Your smile plays like sweet melodies upon my heart strings and your laughter brings back memories of stolen moments where far too many I've missed... but my dreams have kissed your cheeks a million times until these lines seemed familiar. Reoccurring themes have me wishing for things I'm missing like goodnight kisses and long hugs goodbye, wake ups and stay up late at nights and talking and walking in the daylight, holding hands and coming to understand my absence was never the intent. The hurt and pain I caused was never meant it was just a circumstance of unfortunate events. Trials sent that break up husbands and wives, those unforeseen things that changes lives... and I wish I could turn back the hands of time and re-write the song that re-rights the wrongs but my magic faded with the faith lost in your eyes.

Worthlessness would not have me confess that I've lived there for a while, because a father feels worthless to a fatherless child and I could never find the forgiveness to try and heal this brokenness inside so these pains have stayed in my mind and convinced me that forgiveness wasn't worth the time. Repentance for my crimes of misfortune cost me more than any one soul should have to repay. The regrets play like scratched records in my mind etching even deeper the line and wound with each scarred tune that skips its beat, having my hurts stuck on repeat like the constant beating in my chest. I've beaten myself to death and died a thousand times. Through the valleys of the shadow of death to mountains I've climbed just to find peaks of sorrow, plateaus of loneliness and cliffs of regret that heartaches absence won't let me forget and times silence screams violently to remind me that every day is a lesser maybe they'll remember me. Yet I vividly remember times when we all smiled... the small portion of your childhood we shared a while. But how dare I care to get caught in reminiscence... for my fostered thoughts of never presence only recall all the presents I never left and perpetuates the regret of my not being there. It's not like I didn't care, I've cared always. But hurt has strange ways of commanding misunderstanding and I couldn't stand under the demands of a woman scorned, so from my life my pride was torn and my joy was taken. And now for years we've stood unshaken, mistakenly in our stalemate. But hell will have to wait, cause I will break this generational curse.

Here's to hopes for tomorrow...

A concerto billows in my soul for a new day. It sings a symphony of melodies that ring out like Christmas bells and season's greetings at new years. I'm wishing wells of cheer for hopes of seeing you and I draw near. Like Dear John letters in reverse... Let us reverse the curse and begin to heal the hurts because nothing in my life has been worse than this distance between us. If I live to see in us the day you become my best friend I'd only be akin to my father's name. And I pray we'll be the same until the end of time. Until then I'm willing to climb this mountain again to find every treasure hidden in your eyes just to hear you say Daddy again.

GIVE ME A REASON

Inspired by Serenity Poetry's entitled piece

Give me a reason that eases tears in the dark
Give me a reason that draws nearer distant hearts
Give me a reason for lullaby's not to sing of regret
Give me a reason this was something you'll never forget
Give me a reason worth believing when things fall apart
Give me a reason to seemingly dream of a new start
Give me a reason in which to place the faith to carry on
Give me a reason I've been needing all along

CONFESSION #222

Before anyone ever knew I had a poet's soul... they all knew I had a singer's voice. It was easy to allow people to see the singer in me, but the real me lay hidden inside... Unseen, isolated in my mind and often misunderstood. So, more time than less I would rarely express the inner parts of my heart. I kept all of my confessions to myself... until they spilled out upon the pages in pains and heartaches and rages... because My Unsung Soul couldn't hold them in any more.

Here, this soul whom all have heard sing... was bound in chains of silence, anchored by an overwhelming fear of forever being misunderstood. Even in the "in" crowd I stood out. Never did like the same things as everybody else... I just couldn't find the strength in that until years later. I always stood outside the conversation, because what do sports commentators and poets have in common? "Nothing" (other than speaking...). My whole world became the girl, because she, like me, thought more on beauty, elegance, art and the architecture of relations. And I developed a sensational knack for providing her just that thing she most desired. Intimacy... And it, in turn, became an addiction for me... and I've been hooked on it ever since. Hence, the name Unsung isn't a celebration of myself. It's the deep seated part of my character that nurtured me through the trying years of my youth and gave me the strength to be different. And it's made complete by my attaching the word Poet.

I believe there's a little Unsung in all of us...

Loss

My mind...
Made to turn the page
My heart gave way
To what I held dear for too long
My fear grew strong
I knew wrong was to cleave to you
But I hung on till love became my noose
I hang...
Like Southern Trees who bear strange fruit
I bear my soul to you
My bare skin to cross burning sands
Upon hands and knees
I blister and bleed to bear this burden of loving you
It scorches me...
It tortures me endlessly to no avail
My endless love will n'ere prevail...
Weeping willow sing to me
Mocking birds mock me
And despair knocks upon my heart...
It is empty
An echo of sorrow bellows out of the hollow
Ways of my hearts homestead...
Silence in my head
Broken by one thought
A solitary syllable...
Loss

Giving Up

As Inspired by Donny Hathaway

This... This is a soulful moan. Call it a longing for letting go... a groaning for the heartache of holding on to what was over so long ago.

I've often thought of what it would be like to let this love fly away... to die away into distance like ships passing in the night. But try as I might, I haven't found the strength to let you drift into the abyss of my forgetfulness. So, often I'm faced with remembering this...

Giving up is hard to do... when time rewinds in your mind like replays and love races in your heart like relays to constantly remind you of someone... When emotion blankets you like oceans of clover and those hard to let go blues crash over your soul like tsunami waves and wash away the very breath that you depend upon.

Taking away the warmth of what you've grown used to holding close to you... where the mere reminiscence of a kiss and caress are all you have left to cling to... Now love songs sing to you and mean to you so much more than they ever seemed to before, because now they bring you a reminiscent happiness of a loves past begets, but you'd die to forget that loves loss regret and how it resigns you to giving up...

Giving up is as hard as not gasping for one last breath... Not quite the same as giving in, this surrender isn't easy. This burdensome love comes with a cost as heavy as anchor chains bound to your heart. It whispers of never letting go, over and over, like echoes in the hollows of your soul.

I've watched the light in my heart flicker out to darkness... where a wish for a spark to just catch a glinting hint of you brings my soul to hope and my heart to pray... with a faith for enduring love that will chase this pain away... and every time I find the mind to remember you, there's an anguish and pain resilient too... and
Giving up is so hard to do.

TIRED

Troubles came today
With no signs of rain to say
They were coming
Poured down monsoon pains upon me
While the sun shined upon my face
Placed... A wrench in my stomach
And twisted my insides
While I sat by her bedside my heart cried
The faint hint of bile and excrement
Left their scent as a constant reminder
Of the death that crept inside her
A shell of shallow breaths left
Historic skin she sleeps in
Marked like sepia toned road maps
Long naps... She slumbers
Under watchful watered eyes of loved ones
No tears run...
Yet, silent goodbyes begun
I pause to kiss her peaked cheeks
In the place where she lay asleep
Every storm weathered is read
In the lines upon her head
God, bless her tired soul
Soon to trade her silver crown
For a crown of gold
Ne'er would I rush her love away

But trust there is a dwelling place
Awaiting the day to see her face
In God's tabernacle
Her place of safety
Sanctuary and security
To rest assuredly in His presence

BLESSED ASSURANCE

Today came a blessing in her pressing onward
How strong would any have stood in her stead?
Her furrowed brow and silvered head
Now sleep peacefully
No longer burdened
Her chest rests easily
See her cradled in the bosom of Christ
Rejoicing her extraordinary Life
Speaking with the King of Kings
Seeing what eyes have never seen
Nor hath hearts ever imagined
Today came a blessing in her passing
For yesterday's wares of tomorrows cares
Are no more
Now she's reached Heaven's distant shore
Sailed away on yesterday's tears
Into today's sunset
No regrets
All have been cast into forgetfulness
And all that she'd forgotten
There awaits
Her victorious entrance at the gates
As though only moments had passed
Since last they embraced
And once again they see her smiling face
Now embracing everlasting
Today came a blessing in her passing.

BLU

Inspired by Blu Cantrell's "I Can't Believe"

Heart racing
Pacing back and forth
Facing challenges of new days at last
Erasing my past with forgets
My regrets not gone
But no longer clouding my present
Hesitant yet I relent
Consent to live content without you
But lies hide in what hearts denied
Cried inside for breaks sake
Overtaken with inner visions
At the mention of a name
Restrain my wandering
Pondering tomorrows and sorrows of yesterdays
But daily I wake to chasing rays
Casting lights to fading nights
Where dreams break away and take away
All that's left
Reflections of self-revealing feelings
That should have long faded
My heart protested but love betrayed it
Weighted down
Heavy and profound
Trusting but lost in longing
Lonesome without knowing

But hoping to hear again loves soliloquy
Serenade me back to sleep

I pray to keep you, secret, safe.
Kept away from present days
Hallways of memories
Call always to hollow places
And empty wall spaces where frames used to hang
And chandeliers of shame expose my soul
For ever having loved and ever letting go
For ever holding on too long
To what was wrong
Never strong enough to stand long enough
The test of time
Broken promises shattered in mind
Spilling feelings like sands of an hour glass.
Passing fast the moments stolen
Never again to be spoken
Just a token of heartache

And I can't believe
That you've done this
To me.

SAY IT IN SIX WORDS

I write in spite of pain...

THIS IS SPIRITUAL WAR

VICTORY

April 17, 2012 at 2:25pm

Welcome to real life.
Now, hold your noses...
Cause this walk ain't no bed of roses.
As I reminisce memory lane
Traveled there and back again
Too many times to forget the way...
Cause she was my favorite sin
And every time I thought I was out
Her siren's song would pull me back in.
Like a sweet seduction
Corruption set hold in my soul
And turned my Once Upon A Warm Heart cold
When love waxed old
The broken pieces in me released a beast
And I became a fiend of the streets
Addicted to the night
And everything I knew wasn't right
Cause right was where my heart used to be.

Why hast Thou forsaken me?
Now Darkness has overtaken me
Taking me places I don't even wanna be.
Dirty mattresses, dark alleys and backseats
Fiends to tricks to Johns
Pushers to pimps to cons...
Back alley Sally's and motels on I-95...

How am I still alive?
Knowin'... some of the places I used to go in
You could only get in covered in sin.
Admission was the submission of your soul...
You never know...
Or realize just how far you could fall
Until you see yourself being made to crawl
And you tell yourself to get up
But you keep lying down
Until the devil's got your face on the ground
And the only sound that you can hear
Is him in your ear
Telling you "This death was meant just for you."
And you cry "JESUS"
But he says "Jesus ain't down here wit you!
He didn't bring you... He ain't coming back to git you!
You're in my house now...
You came in of your own free will
So, I'm gone steal, destroy and kill
Any dream you ever had of being anything...
Stay down, there's no hope to be seen."

Only God knows the holes my soul has slept in.
Like a pile of crap fresh stepped in
Bodies rotting in doorways...
As I descended staircases to Hell

My soul smelled of fire and brimstone
Like sulfur thrown on one thousand degrees
And the only way up...
Was from on my knees.
But I had to fight to get there.
The shame of my sin kept me from prayer
So, for years I just stayed a slave.
Took solace in my cave of isolation
And let Satan continue to nurture my pain.
In my loneliness he was always there
Watchfully aware...
To make sure I didn't call on Jesus' name.
So he reminded me daily...
How much hurt I was in
In how much dirt I had been
And that the stench of sin was fresh on me
From the bed I'd just climbed out of.
"You smell like sex
She calls it love, but her husband will be home soon...
So, Jesus don't want nothing to do with you."

But I don't really want to do this anymore
I'm tired of walking with my face to the floor...
Pacing this narrow cell
Waiting only to die and go to hell.
So, I remember my life was bought with a price.

Purchased by the Blood of Christ.
I don't have to live in sin anymore
So, keep your pain and shame
I'm out the door.
I'll crawl out if I have to... I crawled in...
But I'm NOT sacrificing another WIN
When I have a Present Help
And if He can love me, I can love myself...
So, I don't need your disgust anymore
I won't need your lust anymore
My heart is longing for a love that Pure...

So, Father, Forgive me...
I know I've fallen far short of your glory
But your grace and mercy's sufficient for me...
So, I come repentantly
Longing only just to be saved
And I pray this prayer in Jesus' name.
Reclaim a sinner like me.

And God said, "It's already done,
Before you were born, I called you, Son
And ordained that your life would bring me glory...
Now, go and tell the world your story.
This is Victory.

A Moment for the Lord

Dear God,

I haven't taken the time today, though I've had the opportunity...
To express how much I love you and what you mean to me.
So, if you would allow me now, just a moment or two...
While it's on my mind and in my heart, to have a word with you.
See, I'm new to the fold, but you took me in... when I was lost and steeped in sin.
You cleaned me up and made me new... and clothed me to look more like you.
Where I was torn, you made me whole... and you forgave and saved my soul.
I can't begin to thank you enough...
When I think of your goodness, your mercy and love...
And how you could be mindful of me... to heal and fill and make me free
When I know, I Oh, so don't deserve it.
You said, I need but to repent... and you would renew a right spirit.
Lord, let your Spirit rest in me... for where the Spirit is, there is liberty.
So, I just want to take this moment Lord, to simply say thank you...
For everything you are to me... and everything you do.
When you woke me up this morning the sun was shining through...
I'm glad my waking days aren't based on my reminding you.
When I opened my eyes and stood to my feet...

I was in my right mind... and able to see... and able to hear... and able to speak,
Because through the night you kept watch over me.
So, I just want to take a moment Lord, to simply say thank you...
For everything you are to me... and everything you do.
You're the source of my strength...and the strength of my life.
You're my comfort and joy... and my peace of mind.
You're the heart of my hope... contentment and might.
You're a lamp to my feet... a flame and a light.
You're my way out of no way... when I cannot see.
You're my Deliverer... my Provider... you're everything to me.
So, I just want to take a moment Lord, to simply say thank you...
For everything you are to me... and everything you do.
El Shadai... Elohim... Addoni... Everything...
Jireh... Rohi... Shammah... Nissi...
Lord, you are more... than enough for me.
But, I can't begin to thank you enough... for carrying me when times get rough...
For guiding my feet safe through harm's way...
For your loving kindness and mercies each day...
For the gift of your Spirit and the gift of your Son...
For you knew I would sin, but he died for each one...
For everything you are to me... and everything you do...
I just want to take a moment Lord, to tell you I love you...
Forever Yours,
Me.

The Other Guy

It's a long way down from here.
One wrong step and I'm done...
I become
The blood stains on the pavement.
This tightrope enslavement
Is killing me slowly.
I'd rather choke and hang
Than continue tip-toeing in this game
Of how to walk softly...
Shackles off me
These eggshells under my feet
Are more than metaphorically beneath me
They bereave me
And leave me speechless.
But preach-less is the price of my silence
I swallow this verbal violence
Bite off my tongue
And let the ink run for my rages' sake.
Each page is soaked
In words I choke on.
But I don't know
How much longer I can hold on...
"...My secret... I'm always angry."
I wanna SMASH everything that pains me
And release the beast that never sleeps... inside
He just hides behind my eyes

Never placing his reputation on the line
I take all the blame.
Condemnation only spoken on my name
And your words don't make my strain any easier.
Take heed of your sanctimoniousness.
You curse in verse as much as you bless
But curb that introspection
See your own reflection...
Detection in retrospect is unheard of.
Casting scripture like stones
Don't speak in love
And if it does
I'd rather be cursed at.
But you won't like me when I'm angry
I curse back...
And my tongue then becomes a guillotine
When how I feel is seen
All who pose a threat better beware
This prose chops like blades through thin air.
"...like a nerve... exposed"
My composure holds still until you touch me
You never shake awake a sleeping beast
Without a song to sing him back to sleep
And the music to soothe his savagery
Before you shake him
You better measure the gravity...
It's a long way down from here.

Spiritual Beast

I used to be grimy but now I'm grizzly
All the Glory be His... See
Cause I'm not the man I used to be.
I once was blind but now I see
How amazing grace saved...
Just a wretched man like me.

See, what was broken is whole again
Now it can be told of him
That potter's testimony that molded him
Folded in open arms
Held like a mothers hug
But it was the Savior's love
That broke the devils hold on him

Liken the Brothers Grimm
His story ain't a tale with a fairy's end
But it tells victory
Cause he was sent to be
The propitiation for every nation of the world to see.

He died for you and me
On a hill called Calvary
Think it coincidence our defense
We call the Calvary?
Warrior soldiers on horses of warfare

But vision dragons and demons at war with angels in the air
Wickedness in high places...
Principalities
To battle these we release them Spiritual Beasts.

That Body armored Teflon
Rhino on a rampage
The Horn of Salvations trumpeteer...
Fall you walls of Jericho
We ROAR everywhere we go
Blow the horn
The sound of war is in the air.

Like that Conquering Lion
His tongues like a two edged sword
Declaring that Spoken Word of the Lord
Ripping scripture in pentameter n' iambic verse
Preaching deliverance to reverse the works of the curse.
Another Beast on the mic!

If these were times of peace we might
Release those poetic melodies that please.
But please believe that this is WARFARE!
It don't get no more fair
Mass murders and destruction are in the air
The times are relevant

The signs are evident
Don't be blind and think that hell is irrelevant,
Cause everybody preaching heaven ain't going.
Just because they came in Jesus name...
Don't mean they know Him.
And these can only be cast out through fasting and pray
So I stay prayed and fasted like that Grizzly Bear
Hibernated in the spirit...
When I wake it's time to feast
Cause I been dreaming bout slaying demons in my sleep.

Now release that beast!
That roars like a thunderous rage!
Somebody said
Who let that Silverback Gorilla out the cage!?
4 The Kingdom!
To be saved from the grave we bring them
Hallelujah Praise Always we sing dem!
Hands raised as a sign of WAR!
Cause we don't pray for Peace anymore!

No weapon formed shall prosper!
I'm more than a Conqueror at War...
Be warned! I'm a Commander for the KING!!!
Eveready to FIGHT!
A Thousand shall fall at my left
And Ten Thousand shall fall at my right!

I'm reliant upon the Lord
Defiant to Satan's hoards
I'm taking back if I have to take it by FORCE!

I'm a demon slayer!
With the Power to speak release
In this spiritual war, I'm a Spiritual Beast!

LUST AT FIRST SIGHT

There's a rhythm in the distance
Drums echo my beating heart
A rhythmic persistence driven to continue beating since its start
Bear in mind it's skipped a beat or two
Palpitated when I first laid eyes on you
Cause I could see poetry in your eyes
And it's amazing...
This stargazing conversation we exchanged in a glance
Got the guards of my heart caught in a trance
And I can't believe this chance we're taking
Cause if I'm not mistaken...
Wasn't that your man?
I guess nothing beats a plan like a better plan...
You're silently speaking to my thinking
Leaving subliminal points of exclamation that resound like rim
shots in my soul
Whispering in explicative...
And my circumstance is indicative of bondage
Because now I'm bound to you
Bound to do what I know better...
Bound to let a look shake the foundations of our relations
Because I was shook when I took one look at you.
So where do we go from here?
I'm caught in a Catch 22
Strawberry Letter 23 plays in my mind
This moment's suspended in time

My whole world moves in slow motion
But I can feel me spinning out of control
Cause you just shifted my axis

Tilted me just a little to the left
And now I can't think right
Created a polar shift in my brain cavity
The loss of gravity has got me floating into the galaxy
And all I'm seeing is stars
Got my head spinning like rings around Saturn
Thinking about your Venus and my Mars
Caught in a glance
And some would say take a chance on love
But I know better...
Cause that ain't ever what this was
This was always... Lust at first sight.

Under Your Anointing

Lord, I thirst for thee
Like antelope for cool springs
Like green pastures for mornings dew
Let me glisten in the light of you
Pour out your sweet Spirit
Fall upon me like rain
Shower me with your presence

And bathe me once again
In your anointing
Yours is the sweetest kiss upon my lips
My soul savor's the taste of praise
Saturate me in reverence, Lord
For the rest of my days
Drench me in my spirit
With a refreshing spritz of you
Wash me with the waters of your love
Make my life anew
By your anointing
Open up the floodgates of Heaven
Let Holy Rivers run
Break upon the shores of my soul
Thy restoration come
Let me drink from the Cup of Your Salvation
Sup from the grapes of your divine
Be filled with the power of your Spirit
And quenched for all of time
Under Your Anointing

A Drug Named She

She...
She makes my mind race
Back to places in time where
We...
We were like piano strings and keys
Meant to be together
Like rose pedals and thorns
Kisses and candlelight
A slow burn and a glass pipe
The one, no good without the other
We...
We were lovers
And I can't forget fast enough
The feeling that her touch begets in me...
So, I... I try with all my might
To fight the fires that She ignites
When with one word
She... Whispers infernos in my soul.
I...
Listen longingly to her distant lovers call
She... Echoes within me
Singing in the hollows of my heart
Her sirens song
And I...
Once again am drawn in.

"Strength is not my story. There's a constant tug in my mind that forever tries to pull me back in time; reminding me of my past habits. She tempts me on a daily basis. Just a little less today than yesterday."

REVERENCE

The Wisdom of a Tree

Our Father,
Which art in heaven
Everything Thou hand hast made
Sovereign and Ancient of Days
Thou art excellent in all Thy ways
Yet, be Thou mindful of me...

Creator of heaven and earth
How marvelous art Thou works
Each masterpiece captures me surprisingly
Sunrise you speak into the skies
Eloquently delicate
Your brushstroke masterfully crafted
In detail that never repeats itself
Your majesty precedes itself
For there is none other worthy
Of announcing your daybreak

I stand silent before your dawn...
Grant me the wisdom of a tree
To bend and bow only unto Thee
To sway only at your leading
To stand firm and deeply rooted by your seeding
Shaped through trial and circumstance
Ever growing in my knowing
That I shall not be moved...

For you have planted me in the greenest pasture
Placed me safely beside still waters
Carefully considered my roots
My branches stretched towards you
In every direction
Is my trunk's praise for your protection
Through these years of letting me grow strong

Placed where I belong...
The wind's whistle though my leaves is my song
To Thee in worship
Perfectly shaped and molded me
Through seasons of change
Blessing me with every rain poured down from heaven
Your floodgates cleanse my soul
From my sapling years
Unto my years of old
I'll be the tree you've created
For only you can make a tree...

Thankful to have shaded all who sat under me
Inspired those who dared to climb higher
Hid the hide and seekers
Hung the dangling sneakers and tire swings...
Sheltered the helpless who've sought solace in my hollows
Gave the wood that fueled the flames of tomorrow

And provided warmth through the night
Until my last leaf falls
At the end of my life
Grant me Thy sweet serenity
And the wisdom of this tree
To reverence Thee
All the days of my life
And I shall dwell
In the house of the Lord
Forever
Amen.

JUDAS WHEAT TESTIMONY

I'm so sick of the hypocrisy
I'm trying not to let it eat at me...
I refuse to become infected with your disease.
Spread like leprosy,
Black plagued telepathy causing dark thought
That brought the black death of me.
I'm trying hard not to enter into darkness again.
I'm trying to keep my mind fixed and stayed on him,
But when I look around
I am confounded by compounded liars,
Compelled to tell their untruths...
And I hear not with my natural ear,
But in how I see the things that you do...
Speaking with forked tongues,
Living double lives.
I won't believe in your pretentious ways or your lies.
And I won't partake of traitorous bread.
I won't allow your inbred
Betrayals to breed in my head.
There is therefore now no condemnation to be fed.
I won't eat your Judas wheat
And reap the starvation that you wrought.
I'd rather starve than eat
The bread that you brought.
I won't become doubled tongued...
There is only me and one speech.

Take it as it is or leave me as I be...
I am content to be unaccepted. (By you).
Acceptable In your sight is not the plight of my life.
You hath no hell to condemn me to.
My soul, will I commend to you?
How can you judge my upright way
When you can't stay in an upright position?
Why sit and listen
To a sermon when you're only concern is hiding the truth...
I won't take part in what you do...
Your hypocrisy only goes so far with me.
I don't mind telling the truth when it hurts
Or telling the truth when it's worse than telling a lie.
That's the freedom that thrives in I.
I hide behind nothing...
When you see me, you see me.
My mask is made of the same skin I was birthed in.
There are no disguises in my life.
I don't dress up, I just get dressed.
And I come through the door as myself.
My, not a perfect man, self.
My, take me as I am, self.
My, you should have seen me
When I was completely covered in sin, self.
My, came to get help, self.
But you can't help me because I don't look like you...

I don't smell like you do.
I don't own expensive perfumes or colognes
That masks the stench of my lifestyle.
I don't wear any long coat suits
To hide the fact that my life's vile
And I need to be seen a certain way
Among the many who dress the same as I do,
Because they live the same lie too.
No, I don't play that sanctimonious game.
My sin repents the same.
So, if I say some ish that offends you,
Then be offended,
And know that I intended to
And didn't pretend it.
Feel free to do the same with me.
Don't speak to me with pleasantries,
Twisting scriptures just to curse at me
In a verse objectively.
Don't collectively pretend to know me
And what I been through,
If you can't show me where your go through
Fell though and how you got through.
My life ain't peace and blessings,
So don't greet me with weak expression...
Sweet confections and salutations of salvation.
Meat me with something real.

Feed me so I can fill.
My hunger pangs refrain my ability to hear you clearly.
I have no use for worthless words.
Tell me something I haven't heard.
What good does your "we were blessed to have you" do me,
If I don't feel blessed to be... here?
I came to see clear,
But all I witness in your witness
To me is pretentious.
I'm supposed to trust you because you look the part?
So does every other con that I know.
You think I can't recognize a fake when I see one?
I used to be one.
All I see done
Is folks putting on a show.
Since you saved your self-righteous self,
Spare me your self-righteousness.
In my eye your right just left.
You surrounded me
When I knelt down to knee...
All praises be to God for saving me,
But where were you when I fell down.
When I was hell bound,
You spoke out but didn't reach out.
So, you shout hallelujah...
And I'll see right through you.

Stained glass's beauty is seen through the light,
But I can't see beauty
Through the windows of your life.
It's too dark inside to see clear.
My visibility drear.
It just looks like shades of broken glass from here.
At least the hotel will leave a light on
And keep the door open
In hopes a stranger'll walk in,
But it aint one church on the block
Whose doors stay unlocked.
I wandered by
Many times and wondered why...
I had to knock so hard to get in.
I had to knock sin.
I have to knock addiction,
I had to knock conviction,
And I had to knock the clothes I wore.
I had to knock the things I said,
The places I laid my head,
Just to get to a place where I could be fed.
Oh, but thank God
I didn't need you before then.
I couldn't walk through your door... then,
But I had Him
To walk the streets with me.

He was there when my sins impeded me...
He came to see me in my jail cell.
He forgave my wrongful ways well
Before I confessed Him in my life convictions.
And He would listen to me speak
Even before I knew chapter: verse.
He won't afraid reach out to me first...
To walk down my side of the street...
He came to where I stayed to visit me.
When my ways were still foul,
I was still a child to Him.
I didn't have to be so clean to be seen...
He meant it when He told me
To come as I was,
And He would give me love.
He gave me all
Of what you didn't give me any of.
You confused my tattoos with treacherous ways...
Tear drops tatted on my face for bloodstains.
You would be misunderstood
In my hood not to have some.
This ink speaks
Where I come from.
It's a testimony...
The blessed are only
The ones who survive.

We'll rest in peace on the other side.
When I tried to confide
In your brotherly love
You couldn't show me the meaning of
What it was that makes you different?
So, I, from here went
To the place where brothers took me in.
Took me in all my sin.
And when I got saved I gave them
The right hand of fellowship.
And now I'm well equipped
To come back to you
And expose you to the truth
Through what I had to overcome.
Prepare for the return of a Prodigal Son.

THIS AIN'T WHAT YOU WANT

Call fire down from heaven
Consume the alter egos
Of these faltered hero's
For none rose
To the occasion
But one
Gave his own eulogy
Hung his head and said
"It is done"
And the earth quaked at his exit
He shook the foundations of Hell
Took the keys from Satan himself
And walked out victorious.
How glorious to call on Jesus...

When I need him
He's a present help
So I'm never by myself
Though I roll solo
My dough-lo needs nobody else
And we can either fight or pray.
I'm a warrior for the King
Yeah, that means I throw blows both ways.
Don't ever take my God for no chump...
And you better know for show'

Daddy didn't raise no punks.
Mind ya manners when you see me
Just in case my "speak easy" ain't what it should be
Don't have to be reminded I'm from the hood "B"
I left the game... The game didn't leave me
So mind you, I ain't forgot how to...
Without a shadow of a doubt
I can be bout you
Lights out you...
Never knew what hit you
Better I getcha with scripture

Than have to lay hands that befits your
Mistaken identity
Cause you must have mistaken me
For someone else.
Better write a letter to self
I ain't that "turn the other cheek" type Christian
I was made for war.
Enough said
Need I say no more
Cause you don't wanna see that Gorilla...
Another thriller in Manila
Be we don't rope-a-dope
We go for broke
So blow for blow I go beast mode.

You looking at Gorilla Warfare
Should have took more care
Before to beware
And not let this smooth mood fool ya
Hate to have to school ya
But class is in session
This lesson is worth learning from someone else
Don't make it harder on yourself than it has to be
I make a masterpiece of catastrophe
And it would be a tragedy
To learn the hard way
And not the smart way
But so long as you learn from the mistake.
I ain't the one.

COVER ME

Lord, let me hide myself in thee
Place me in thy cleft and cover me
Let me look out over cliffs of controversy
And see clearly the paths you've lain for me
Let my foot dash not against the rocks
Nor burn in deserts sands
For years of wanderings
Provide the premise for my ponderings
That my mind is fixed and stayed on thee
That I might walk waters to cross borders for your glory.

It is a light thing for you to part the sea
Speak peace to the storm and it shall cease
As much as I believe these things that thou hast said
Let me have faith to raise the dead
And speak to mountains
Be thou cast into the sea
For this is the power that God has given me
And I am not a wonder,
But just a subject who's under his divine anointing
His assigned appointing
To be a King and a Priest
Granted the power to speak release
And manifest destiny

As I confess in the prophetic
My testimony will reach
Teach and set free
Those enslaved to spiritual captivity
And break the chains of their yesterdays.
Show them better ways in Christ Jesus
And let this Jesus piece ease us into conviction
That leads us to submission
And frees us into repentance, salvation and grace

Lord, place me in that secret place
And let me hide-away in thee
As I cry away my yesterday's release
For the sake of my tomorrows.
Cast my sorrows into thy sea of forgetfulness
Along with my mistakes and my regrets
For I have yet to see your sparrow beg for bread
And I know that my soul shall be fed
By the Word and Living Waters of your truth
Drawn from your fountain of youth
My hope springs eternal
Forever rests in my future
As I ever press towards you,
I look to the mark for the prize of your high calling
Though angels are fallen round about me
Thy high praise keeps me safely tucked away

And I am wrapped up in thee.
And my soul sings Hallelujah
Holy, Holy, Holy...
For you are sovereign God
And you are the only
From everlasting to everlasting.
So I count it small my asking
Faith the size of a mustard seed
And strength as rooted as thy tree
Let me stay firmly planted in thee
And bring forth an abundant fruit
Let me only speak thy truth

Teach me thy ways that I might prove
What is that good and acceptable way of the Lord
Let my life shine bright in the night of the world
And draw men for days unto thy ways
Not my will but thy will be done in me
That Christ-like is all I aspire to be
Father, shape me
Mold and make me...
Break me into thy image if need be
Oh, how I need thee
Always

Cover me in thy glory, yet hide thy face
As I am yet unworthy to look upon thy countenance
Teach me your ways
As I walk through doorways that thou hast prepared for me.
Be a light unto my path...
A lamp unto my feet
And let me run swift this race you've placed before me.
Unto you be glory
Honor... Dominion and power
Now and forever
Amen.

THE MASTER'S PIECE

I think best in ebony, but indigo will do
My most vivid compositions were all painted in black and blue
Let me paint a picture written in red...

How splendid is the imagery
I can see the symmetry taking form
The balance in composition
As words fall in position
And I'm filling in the negative space
I begin to see a four pointed star taking shape...
Its light is amazing
It illuminates the page in a way that makes shading sinful
Still...
I have a pen full of ink
To make splotches and drops
Tittles and jots of details
Dark spots to see well
The story that this painting tells

They say a picture's worth a thousand words
At least that what I've heard...
Maybe I'll entitle this piece
A Crown of Thorns...
If I called it Salvation
Would your imagination
Run like crimson tides

Down the pierced side of my Savior?
Or do you favor
A red line in a blue sky?

How is it that you've come by
This gallery of listening?
What you're witnessing is a miracle.
A Lyrical Movement in the spiritual.
A portrait of His saving grace
Can you see the Saviors face?
Envision His body stretched
Till every joint was out of place?
See the agony in His eyes
Hear
The desperation in His cries
Feel the heartache in His mother's final goodbye
See the injustice that runs in red
Feel the hatred in the words written above His head
As he hung his head
And died on a cross.
Let me paint a perfect picture...

I AM MORE

I am more than the sum of my parts. I would not take away any one part of me to be replaced with what hasn't made me who I am. I would not trade one pain for laughter or one inconvenience for gain. That's not to say that if I had it to do all over again; I'd do it exactly the same. It's only to say that I wouldn't trade away the experiences I've gained, for I am more than merely the sum of my parts.

I am stronger than my weaknesses would have me perceived. Though I've cried streams of fallen tears over the years, my weakness is only human. I'm not impenetrable or immune in this world's hurts. I would not have this heart to be so guarded that I'm invulnerable to its breaking. And I have taken steps towards temptation as much as any man and found it hard to stand under my own convictions. But through it all I've been strengthen in my weaknesses and I am more than they will ever label me.

I am more knowledgeable than the years of education I've amassed and wiser than the streets that raised me. I've been classed, graded and GPA'ed, rewarded, honored and praised, but no scholastic arts accolade will ever define my identity. No credential will truly speak of me. I've found more value in lessons I learned in the street than book smarts earned in a university and still I am more than their combined wisdoms will ever tell of me.

I am more compassionate than pains of loss would like me to be and more forgiving than my broken heart believes. I'm more willing than reluctant in my ability to love and more patient than my frustrations speak of. It is a challenge to temper disappointments and curb the regrets of being let down. It's a fight not to become hard hearted by endings that never should have started and beginnings that seem only to begin again and again and again and again, seemingly never to obtain a gain, only to remain the same and I'm tired of starting over. How many times must we say the same things before we explore what tomorrow brings?

I am more daring than my precautious tendencies. I'm more accepting to change. I've learned through humility that nothing stays the same and nothing worth having comes easy. So, my comfort zones no longer impede me and I'll jump in spite of a fear of falling, for having placed greater faith in the belief that I'll succeed. I am more than what failures or fears have called me.

I am more faithful a friend in absence than distance says I've been. I am more than what you can't see.

I'm more serene than my temper makes me out to be and more refined than my rugged demeanor. When you look at me, my eyes speak the depths of a soul that's grown through every suffering and circumstance, and it's not by chance that I am more...

WHEN COMES PEACE

When wonderings have left me
all alone
feeling misunderstood
and I find my standing
in solitude
for those who
once stood with me
have all moved on
Then comes peace...

He comes and reminds me
that solitude has always been
where he finds me
That feelings of isolation
and loneliness
come only as
reminders
to once again lean upon him
for no strength be found in any of them
He gives me peace...

When this strength wanes within me
my heart pains me so
like chest wounds opened long ago
that never healed
completely

I look to him to entreat me
to peace...

When for slumber
sleep never comes
and midnight hour till daybreak runs
I lay awake
pondering the meanings
searching for lines of clarity
what defines the definitive me
for what cause
for what reason
was thus created a season of suffering
for such a time as this
I beseech thee
reprieve me
My fettered soul need be freed
This gift come as a weight to carry
give me wings
to marry the wind
to a spoken testimony confession of sin
Let soar these sorrows
for tomorrows sake
take away the tethers
dissipate the clouds that weather above me
when dreary falls

Hear
my weary calls
and find me
Peace...

WEAPON OF PRAISE

My Testimony Part 3

Enemy mine lies like land mines in sand waiting to trip...
Ripping shrapnel in my side...
Spitting dirt in my eyes...
Thinking I can't see THEM as I pass by.
These haters on elevators that only move sideways,
Super highways to nowhere.
I didn't want to go there,
Cause it takes me low there...
But they need to know their days are numbered with me.
Remember with me a time when we were friends...
I didn't see that we were enemies then,
And I would have been none the wiser...
Had ENEMY LIES actually been the truth.
Foolishness of my youth...
Like childish things I put away.
Now the wisdom of the WORD is here to stay.
Prove me here this day...
If God be for me, who can be against me?
Who, be you, to fence me?
I war, infinitely... to set captives free...
First captive was me...
But no shackles hold me now...
My breakthrough praise raised me somehow.
It took a little while...
My dark wasn't trying to find the light.

I had to praise the darkness out my night
So my life could see brighter days.
His ways are not our ways...
He had to break me down to take me to a higher place.
But broke me and remolded me...
Holded me enfolded He... said BEHOLD, IS HE... ALL THAT I SAID
HE'D BE...
AND MY WORD SHALL NOT RETURN UNTO ME VOID.
Spoke into my destiny...
Before my conception He...
Ordained me a weapon for the Lord.
A DRAGON SLAYER,
Fire breathing prayer...
A yielding shield of faith hands layer...
A whole armor bearer...
A wearer of robe and crown...
And when praise goes up, HE REIGNS down.
Anointed me appointedly...
A King and a Priest.
My Sword and Cross both slay the beast...
His Word and His Blood...
His Power and His Love...
If by our testimony we shall overcome,
I'll testify until the day I die.
He saved me...
The Light He gave me shines like a beacon for all to see.
I AM a weapon of Praise.

SOUL OF THE NIGHT

Oh, why not?
Its dark and hot... and I'm confined by this body.
These walls of flesh can't deny me.
Let's take a flight into night.
Black Angel come nigh...
Be my dark peace and fly...
Me to a place away from everything familiar.
I have no inhibitions when I'm with you
And we can do...... anything.
Wrap me in black wings and ravish as you will...
All that I have to give.
Take it...
Don't let me go... strip me naked.
Till I'm empty... take every drop of me.
Enfold me in arms of angelic embrace.
Spiral stairways to heaven...
Intertwine thy thighs and mine and let's climb.
Fly me away.
There waits a place where we lay
And I, like serpentine fire, burn desire...
Deep inside of you...
What else shall we do other than make Love?
I'm enraptured in the hold of...
The Soul of the Night.
A spirit called
Passion.

War of the Tongue

From the Prodigal Series

I refuse to be put into a box... Have psychological locks placed on me like Lauryn said. "I get out." There's a war going on inside my head. To fight it out, I write it out... but whited-out pages won't express my rages, so I pose my prose and wage this war of the tongue. Battle speaking what I believe in, my ministry begins... with WAR... and ends with FARE thee well. And all in WAR is FAIR, so, prepare ye hell for my weapon of praise. My WARFARE has violent ways... of silencing my enemies. My sword's my mouthpiece... I chop heads off with the truth and see a headless you. You better pray when you don't know what else to do.

My tongue, when fully loaded... automatically explodes in prayer. Giving utterance to tongues out of nowhere. Slaying in the Spirit... Hear it, but do not understand... This language is known by no man. My nomadic sabbatical... somatically radical... search for inner peace, brought me back to feast, my platter full. My Cup runneth over... my soul is won. My testimony told is one... of prodigal oldest son. But never let go this one... He holds this one in hand. He rose just one as plan... He sent one just to show he knows the intent of man. Now, just as I am, come. Sit, like cloven tongues... Gust, as a mighty rushing wind where it blows from... nobody knows. My frows and throughways' know high and low days. Lost souls go both ways, so my steadfast and strays know repentance and praise.

Relentlessly persistent and fiendishly resistant met at a crossroads called Calvary and fought for me. My thoughts would be wrought with merciless condemnation and perilous resignation if not for the salvation the Savior bought for me. Thoughtfully, what my cost ought to be, He already paid. Brought the keys of Hell and Death back from the grave... and saved a sinner like me. Now, my soul is free and my story told is Victory.

This war descriptively depicted in my mind subliminally... given visions to be seen as dreams... I walk in my sleep on higher plains. No planes fly as high as I have gained... access in the recesses of my mind. I've seen success divine... and the cessation of holy nations at war... combine. Arch angels and dark angels in spiritual fight... at war in the heavens of my spiritual sight. Now, my plight to share... this vision of spiritual warfare... My fight's in every page I write. My rage, outright commands my pen in hand... His blood He gave to save from sin a man... He raised three days from then again... my debt repaid completely when... my knees be bended... My soul repented... and my heart relentlessly sought His peace. My father's arms opened up to me. Hold me like I never left... made me be my better self... gave me keys to free somebody else with my testimony. So speak release in your life in this ink that I write... I propose to know the woes of no one. This prose is a war of the tongue... but He is faithful to complete that which He begun... so my prayer for our lives is His will be done.

DECADENCE

Come to me
like the lover you're doomed to be
Take cover,
you've run from me long enough

My embrace
ever to be locked around the cuff
fatedly joined at the wrist
indelibly enslaved to a tryst
Found to be
forever bound to me...

What are these thoughts you keep?
Images seeping into your mind
Eros pleasures
you thought you'd left behind
but my secrets to keep hidden
are forbidden thee
so I intimately invade your memory
and orgasm your mind

Crawl to me
down these darkened hallways
come to me upon bended knees
Do beg my pardon
for parting ways so suddenly
but didn't I utterly leave you pleased?

Self-indulgence is so seductive
Shall we indulge indeed?
Come dance this entranced rumba with me
I shalt not be denied
You shall not chastely erase me back to past lives
mistakenly forsaking all we've become
from thence to come hither,
what we've begun

Synergism of phallic
Chalice lust relinquished
Love unrequited
A requiem of decadence incited
A forbidden kiss ensued
Fires of lust ignited
A soul subdued
How dare you
act as if I never knew you

NOW CALL IT TESTIMONY

A Love/Hate Letter

I'm sick of being disciplined
What I've written was expected of me
Dare I raise your level of expectancy?
Dare I to write words that ignite
The parchment of mediocrity in your life?
Care I set fire to the pages
And fan the flame that rages inside of me
When I can't find the form in what you call poetry
And my standard is constantly being raised...

I'm tired of reading page after page
Of the same thing
It's like the squeaking of a broken box spring
It's like old people speaking on Charlie Brown
"Wa wa wa waaa waa"
That same annoying sound
Stuck on repeat
And please don't mistake this for a critique
I'm just speaking what's seeping through my mind...

Apparently poetry is just line after line
Of whatever pops into your head
So I could fit my foot into this piece with ease
Because I'm looking at my toes as we speak...
But are we speaking
Or are you just reading random thoughts
From inside my head?

Dare we identify an audience?
Is it only those who know me by name?
Is it only they who understand my broken slang?
Need you know me personally
To relate to my spoken word?
Or shall a message be clearly heard
Between each line?
These questions ring in my mind
When trying to find the voice to share with the world.

Play time is over.

Wayward Behaviors unto Repentance

Some days are stranger than others
Some days I find it hard to contain this silent rage
A Beast angers inside of me
Nothing sleeps well in a cage
Release me
War is to be waged

What wickedness this way comes
Comes from within...
Like vomit
Regurgitated the taste for sin
And evil is ever with me
When would to do good
I did not
Overtake me now
Forsake not

Forgive me Father for I have sinned
It's been a day since my last confession...
Lost again in a forest of sin
This timber hinders my direction
Lead me to Cedars of Lebanon

I pray to see your reflection in still waters
Let thy peace restore my broken borders
Grant me thy serenity

At ease the beast
That my prey turns into prayers
And my praise released
As a sweet smelling savor unto thee.

SEND ME, LORD

Is it just me or does no one else seem to get it?
Does it not bother anyone else or have I just let it
Get to me in a way that needn't to be?
Have I taken this thing too seriously
Cause all I'm finding is jokes
And the laughter thereafter isn't mine...
Their after lines undefined
When I'm searching for meaning
At a specific place in time
Because these steps are ordered ever forward
Onward pressing
It's a blessing to have direction
But traveling distances with resistance
Requires a constant persistence
And kicking against the pricks
Seems as hopeless as Sisyphus rolling boulders uphill
Why can't I appeal to intellect?
Why is it taken as disrespect to ask for more?
I guess it's just something I'm looking for
That can't be found in my present surroundings
Higher callings resounding
Forsake me not for sakes of others
Commissioned to strengthen my sisters and brothers
When again I'm returned
Better ways for better learned
Forbearing burdens of misunderstanding

Thy command a stand in my demanding
A demonstration unto excellence
For Excellent is thy name
And nothing living ever stays the same

And we've been given a Living Word
Orchestrated and ordained in Glory
To speak life through Victorious Testimonies of overcoming
My spirit is over running with Living waters that flood my soul
And I'll break levees 4 The Kingdom overflow
Cipher cinders sit on my tongue
I can't contain it; my restraint is flaming
Like a Fiya breathing, heat seeking demon destroyer in His name
And I'm proclaiming crowns upon every ground my foot shall tread
Tell every demon in hell I'm taking heads
Beware! My Profession is Warfare!
I've got the heart of a Spartan... I'm startin' WARS
Battle raging; my tongue's a two edged sword
Piercing precision to the division of soul and flesh
I cut asunder to saunter brokenness
Speaking healing and deliverance
Repentance unto forgiveness
And condemnation unto Salvation
I AM come to set captives free
This is a spoken testimony
"I" must go forth if I must as "Only"

Let this cup pass from me?
No... I'm ready to do thy will
Lead me through hell gates to Calvary's Hill
And march an army of Spiritual Beasts beside me
Let your Glory cloud guide me and we shall not know defeat
No retreat for the wicked, they must be slain
And we remain victorious in Jesus name

Is it just me or does no one else seem to see it?
Am I like Sisyphus, doomed to repeat it
Again and again
And again
And again...

Thirty Pieces

For 30 pieces Judas traded in my Jesus
And gave me 30 reasons to write this.
One... Because I AM.
And I would not be had Jesus not died for me...
Death would be my promise for eternity.
Two... For each of His nail-scarred hands...
For the Three days He took to rise again...
He could've done it in one,
But behind the scenes work was being done...
For the Four corners of the Cross.
For the Five points of piercings from which He bled
And for the Six letters that make up the Words in red... G.O.S.P.E.L.
Gospel.
Seven, for being Faithful to complete that which He began
And seeing Salvation through to the end...
Eight... for new beginnings.
For taking the keys of Death and Hell
And taking the stripes from a Cat of Nine tails...
And for the Ten precious words of prayer
He prayed for you...
"Father, forgive them for they know not what they do."
For The Lord's Prayer.
For taking the time to think of me on Calvary
For the thorns on His head and the nails in His feet...
For the spear in His side and the time He cried
"My God, why hast Thou forsaken me?"

For staying on the cross
When at any given time He could've come off
But instead He hung His head and died for me.

Eighteen... for John 3:16 and 17.
For the only perfect life the world has ever seen.
For being a perfect being...
For understanding and overcoming...
For living waters over running my Soul
For never letting go...
For ascending high yet looking low.
For paying the price of what my cost ought to be
For the Salvation that He Bought for me
For going to Hell and setting the captives free
And keeping the keys!
And for Victory in His name over the enemy!

I just gave you 30 Pieces of Praise to trade in for Jesus.
30 reasons of why He's worthy of your believing
And the only thing you had to do to receive Him...
Is confess with your mouth and believe in your heart
That He is the True & Living Son of God...
Who died on a cross... and rose in three days...
Who gave His life that you might be saved...
Accept Christ...
He's already paid the price.
You don't have to Crucify Him again.

Break the Chains

I keep hearing... "You're not made for material gains...
We're not put here for earthly riches"
Like those are my only this world wishes... houses, cars and money galore
"That's not what we were put here for...
We were made to serve the will of the Lord..."

And every scripture in the world has been explored
Or should I say exploited
To make a testament of a lesson YOUR life's avoided
Cause you can barely afford to pay attention
And you never fail to mention how your bills can't get paid on time
"But render unto Caesar what is his...
Give an offering unto the Lord
And unto God you know you owe a tithe"

You've been charged to feed the hungry
Care for the poor and protect the elderly
But seldomly have you ever done any
Randomly patted your pocket for pennies in your passing by
But you never looked that homeless hand directly in the eye
So quit preaching to me!
I'm DOING the reaching you need to be
The wealth of the wicked laid up for the just was speaking to ME
Cause I'm ABOUT my Father's business
To this I will attest
I GIVE and LIVE abundantly blessed!

There's a pounding in my chest
That pushes passion personified
A beating in my bleeding heart to survive
The mundane reality
That society tries to grapple me with
I'd rather be hanged, strangled and whipped
Than made a slave to piety, and self-righteousness
Your right just left when speaking to me

I'm equipped with a gifting
That's Kingdom strengthened and
Spiritually uplifting
And I won't be swayed or persuaded
By your naysaying ambiguities
And since I'm the one pursuing these Visions and Dreams
Do me a favor and spare me the obscurities.

Yeah, you can wrap it in a scripture...
But I can paint a picture with words
To un-curse every verse you ever slurred
I'm a walking weapon of Warfare
How dare you try to judge my heart?
I been reppin' The KINGDOM from the very start
And it's about to get dark in here...
I'm pulling down power lines till blackout
You just let that SILVERBACK... OUT!

Now the pleasantries come to an end
Cause I ain't politically correct
I'm spiritually direct
When I speak 4 The Kingdom
I'm going IN!

And you can try to flip this
But I'm about to rip this UP
The Parable of the Talents to Script this up
Was the Lord's way of saying
Multiply that with which you've been blessed
Give me more than you were given or settle for less
Complacency is a demon
Bound to the Principality of Poverty
I AM come to set the captive free
Jesus said "Follow me"
Are you gone beg at the gate your whole life?
Or are you gone finally stand up and fight?
The healing is in the revealing
Open your eyes... see for yourself
At times we all need a little help
But you gotta participate in your own rescue
Stay down if you want to
Or learn to see beyond your circumstance
My God is an awesome God
And moreover everyday
He's a God of second chance

SCRIPTURED HAIKU... 8/30

For this I besought
Thrice, asking of Jehovah
Take this thing from me.

SCRIPTURED HAIKU... 21/30

Now persuaded I
Shall not be separated
From the love of God

DEATH AND LIFE 24/30 [COUPLET]

I would that life could never end
Our debt to pay the price for sin

For gates to part and enter in
We breathe new life through heavens wind

Death came to take away the pain
And Life through death began again

Forever lasting
For Everlasting

SCRIPTURED HAIKU 25/30

But nevertheless
Not my will, but thine, be done.
In Heaven and Earth

REDEMPTION

From within this lurking has me
calmed and quieted
Silent yet beastly longings to be released
He sleeps inside
Ages passed since last he wandered
She wonders aimlessly by
Her frame to claim
He needing beastly feeding for fiendish pleasures
She measures up
He Eros, his arrows pierce her heart
They lay playing in the dark
Dripping seditions, switching positions
derision of hedonism...
She pleading fear of daybreak
wondering how much more she can take
till mourning comes for grievous mornings
Mirrors made to repent
Nights laid in soiled sheets spent
Heavy laden sighs weighted with bated breaths
She waited till he slain upon her breast
In her bosom lay regret that never left
Upon his chest, a beast that never slept
Lascivious abyss
thy depths descend upon my soul
drawing me dauntingly close to hellish black holes
and seats of sin

When I think I'm out she pulls me back in
Honeycombed and honeysuckled me
with wild berries and Silk she devours me
Showers of confections and sugar selections
drip me in warmth
Covered me buttery brown toasted buns of perfection
and fed me breakfast in bed.
Dream schemes run through my head
Memories calling me to a fallen he
I stood once... Soon once more
My ever haunting is just behind closed doors.
She calls me, Pornography
For longed breaks of fidelity's sake
Her thrust of lust appeases me
And I'm easily reminded of times I'd fine
places of refuge in faces of shame
And houses of ill repute
Dark corners and back doors, mattress on dirty floors
Knowing she never loved me and I never needed her to
We only came to do what we came to do
I don't care if you understand how dark my days were then
I never played my heart over my hand
and every card I dealt myself kept coming up Aces
Royal faces to straight flush
My winners never met beginners luck
cause she was struck by a silver tongue

She married, we indeededly snuck
Indebted to lust, I continuously lived in sin
The darker the night the deeper I faded within
Condemnation to my soul
Heaven's Light, I knew I'd not behold
It was just that I be a slave to lust
cause love couldn't live here anymore
So I suffered she and many more
in ways of monetary chains... exploited
Strip poles and hole in the walls
Hooker strolls and parked cars
Me and the devil started building an army

of sin sick degenerates
Made slaves for generations to come
They all paid and I spared none
But heavy weighed the soul of the man
to this come from where I began
and the Spirit held to a glint of light
And to those who didn't know
It takes but a hint of glow to illuminate the night.
But God placed a spark in my hardened heart
and gave me a mind to return to whence I start
in my Father's house my Saul days were changed
upon my return he estranged my prodigal name
and separated me for himself

a shared inheritance of his wealth
Again he called me son. Said my journey had just begun.
He told me to walk... I wanted to run
But he assured me the race was already won
Be steadfast in the anointing
Your appointing was for such a time as this
I've made you a fisher of men to teach men to fish
Given you nets of testimony
blessing of confessing and praise
I've poured my Sprit upon you for the length of your days
I can only show you tomorrows... I've erased your past
and I've made you first where hurt made you last.
Trust in Me, Thy Redeemer

Power for Living

So this piece....
Though it took me seven days to write it
I'll probably recite it in the designated seven minutes or less
But I bet it's gone bless ya.
You might not like how its tests ya
See, I'm taking off the gloves. I'm coming at cha
Cause I just ain't afraid to keep in real
So I can't be afraid of how you feel
Cause you've been pacified long enough.
They told me always speak the truth in love
But I've kinda had a problem with that.
Because if it's the truth... then IT'S THE TRUTH!
And if how I speak it offends you...
Then maybe you needed to be offended
Cause I'm sick and tired of your pretending
Tired of Tip-toeing around your feelings
Cause your ego is as big as your sin is
And... you don't want to repent
You're constantly edging God out
And your only fear is that you'll be found out.
Like Hell only lives in your imagination
I'm telling ya... Keep testing His patience
This Grace dispensation is gone end
And you gone reap the wage of sin.
It's a spiritual principle
The seed you sow is the seed you grow

And you ain't planted oranges to get apple trees
So, why you expecting roses when you planted weeds?

Deal with it!
I told you I'm coming REAL with it
Will I be offended by how you feel with it...?
NOT AT ALL!
Cause this seven minutes
Might be the only seven minutes that I get
To hit you with something you won't forget.
I wanna BURN a word from God into your hearts
Hit you with it like hot grits
So it sticks and leaves marks everlasting...
Cause my scars are just healings from my past, when...
Hurt was all I had to show for it.
And I hope it keeps you connected.

So this piece... ain't what I expected...
I thought I was gonna talk about my walk with Christ
Like how I let Him lead my life
But... most of my living's been sinning
So let me tell it from the beginning
I haven't always walked with Christ
But He's always had His hand in my life...
Protected since I was molested
And that was at the age of six

And I've been sexing ever since
Lost innocence changed my life.
But I recognize the hand of Christ
Because it didn't have to turn out alright...
I spent years living in silence
Mastered a mental violence that perpetuated itself in anger.
He knew I was in danger,
And gifted me to find peace of mind
So I learned to pass time thinking in rhyme
Inking lines upon pages that expressed the rages
That plagued my childhood with migraines...
Mind pains hidden in memories...
That didn't want to stay repressed
So, in my silence... my pen confessed.
And he kept me connected.
Respected my parents most of the time
But at 18 I figured this life was mine
And I could do with it what I pleased.
So I became an addict and a fiend
A master manipulator in the sex scene...
Pimpin was my thing
Turned girls out for dollars
Became a scholar of the streets
Tricks and johns... pimps and cons
Knew my name; I ran deep in the game.
It all changed the night I'm looking in the eyes

Of a 21yr old lost soul with a gun
It was a loaded situation.
I couldn't bring balance to the equation
Guess my life had too many variables
But gifted me as a scribe to script these parables...
So you can parallel a life of deliverance

Have I been saved ever since?
Naw!... I still turned and walked away
I took solace in the darkness of Lot's cave.
Sorrow became my friend
I was just another Broken Man...
Broken-hearted, a broken home, a broken mind
I walked the streets of sin on the broken line.
Broke pockets, I broke family ties and broken mirrors
To keep from looking in my eyes.
The waters of my soul were polluted
But He brought me back from the brink...
Just to prove he was the undisputed
Heavyweight Champion of Salvation.
Said "Now, raise a nation."
With this Power of the Tongue demonstration
Power for living keeps being my motivation.
Inspiration fell on... from the words of an Andra Kellon
And I recognized in him my twin
A kindred spirit gifted to spit these lyrics of deliverance

And we been repping the Kingdom ever since.
One brother to another
One Knight... one Iron Man
One more link ⌐ The Kingdom till we stand
One Nation strong
And God knew He'd do it all along
So I Thank Him for keeping my life connected.
This is Power for Living
Amen

How Good God Is

Now some say He's marvelous and marvel at how many miraculous things He's done, never minding that in His ordinary being He's Father, Spirit and Son. Extraordinarily awesome... magnanimous great... and when I think about how good God is I can't exaggerate. The best I could do is to begin to spit this verse in tongues, but then you wouldn't understand where I was coming from, so let me try to put it into words. My God is the most awesome voice to ever speak a spoken word. He spoke light out of darkness... life from death... he spoke abundance when it won't none left and His breath brought dust to life. He's Amazing. Omnipotent Almighty... and if that ain't enough to impress you... Well Alrighty. Let me continue this menu of accolades... cause I could lay it on the line all day and not say the same thing twice. Besides the fact that He gave you life, let me just list what He did for you last night... He spoke breath into your windpipe, told you lungs to act right, controlled your throat so you didn't choke in your sleep, all while keeping your blood flowing without your mind knowing, so you didn't have to think to tell yourself to breathe. He gave you the autonomy to feel like a real boy when He could 'a made you a Pinocchio instead... cause everybody that laid down last night didn't get back up out of bed. You got wood in yo head if the use of yo legs, you think is guaranteed... but He woke you with the use of your limbs and your minds activity... rather than leaving your body lumped in it's catatonic sleep state, where the loss control of your bowels and your bladders contents became the place that you lay. My God is a keeper... He kept you through your last night's dreams... cause the back of yo eyelids

256

really could 'a been the last thing you ever seen. But He woke you up to a beautiful day, even if it's raining outside... cause seeing the rain reminds me I still have the use of my eyes.

...to be continued

One Sovereign God

For every Word you've ever heard
For every sentence said
For every message read between the lines
There is but One Truth.
One Divine...
Who need only be defined by one name.
GOD!
And there is only one.
He's hidden in every crevice of the earth
Revealed in the details of life
There is no place too low or too high
For His hand to reach or His eye to see.
He's remained the same throughout Eternity...
Sovereign!
His name is GOD!
And there is only One...
He reigns Supreme
The OMNIPOTENT Being
Master and Creator of EVERYTHING!
From dust to diamonds
Whatever's spoken from His tongue BECOMES...
And He can speak ANYTHING!
EVERYTHING He says is DONE
For He is SOVEREIGN!
His name is GOD!
And there is only ONE!

Fear Him reverently
Everything in Heaven bows on bended knee...
How sufficient is your Praise to one so worthy
Where Heaven cries HALLELUJAH!
HOLY... HOLY... HOLY
He is SOVEREIGN!
His name is GOD!
And He's the ONLY!...
Our Father which art in Heaven...
Hallowed is His name!
The source from whence my Savior came!
Nobody Greater!
Name another who could've created us a Savior
And gave His only Son...
Everything He says is DONE!
He is SOVEREIGN!
His name is GOD!
And there is only ONE!
Timeless!
With Him there is no end...
He was here before TIME even began!
So, NOTHING in time defies Him...
Even HELL obeys His will!
At His command the OCEANS STAND STILL!!!
WHATEVERS spoken from His tongue BECOMES...
And He can speak ANYTHING!

EVERYTHING He says is DONE!
He is SOVEREIGN!
His name is GOD!
AND THERE IS ONLY ONE!!!
Place no one and no thing above Him
Stand to your feet and raise a PRAISE if you love Him
Cause this piece is almost done
I say again...
He is SOVEREIGN!
His name is GOD!
AND THERE IS ONLY ONE!!!

PRAISE GOD!

The Overtaking

Silverback Gorilla Warfare General of the troop
God's spiritual henchman
In warfare I'm known to lyrically lynch men with the word of God
I hang'em high and hit'em hard
Leave'em swingin I'm rippin these demons apart.
You won't like me when I'm angry
You'll like my pen even less when its mad
I'm like the toughest piece of meat you ever had
Hard to swallow
I'm that lump in your throat
The words you choke on

100 Proof
And I ain't spittin' nothing but the truth.
A spiritual mercenary taking heads
Tongues as sharp as a razors edge
I rightly divide the word of truth
I hunt the walking dead and they look like you
Come MERE!!!
My Mortal Kombat's combating for your immoral soul
This war was waged from days of ole
Cast out of heaven
Your strongman is the one who came back with seven
And made you guilty by association
You didn't take the time to realize
That some of your so called friends have red eyes
And a spirit of divination
They keep your relationships in chaos
Wit dat he said she said...
Séancing your spirit
Listening with your natural ear you won't hear it
So here it is...
That spirit of silence named secret
Told you to keep it to yourself
He whispered... "Don't tell no one else" into your soul
When you were only six years old
And you've been holding on to secrets ever since
The evidence is in your silent tears

I know, cause I cried in silence for years
With Silence came the spirit of Fear
And the spirit of Shame...
And they called on another spirit by the name of Blame Yourself
They wouldn't let me listen to anyone else
Until a spirit named Hurt came along
And Hurt made me weak
I called it Broken Hearted
But then came Pain
And Pain made me strong
At least that's what I thought...
But demons do what they've been taught
They operate in deceit and work well together
See, Pain and Hurt... They always dwell together
One whispers "Always"
And the other yells "Never"
They're very clever and it's hard to sever the twain
And along with Fear, they always call on Anger...
Now you're no stranger to demonic attack
Danger is an ever present fact
Because Anger becomes the leader of the pack
And he expresses himself in RAGE!!!
His THOUGHTS have violent ways
They PLAGUE your MIND with memories and MIGRAINES!
Like RAZOR BLADES in your brain
ICE PICKS AND JABBING PAINS

AND IMAGES THAT YOU ONLY WANT TO FORGET
INCREASING THE PAIN OF REGRET
KEEPING A CONSTANT POUNDING IN YOUR CHEST
UNTIL THE VEINS ARE POPPING OUT OF YOUR HEAD AND YOUR
NECK
AND IF I EVER GET MY HANDS ON YOU!!!
LORD KNOWS... What I might do...
That's why, Lord
I gotta give this Anger up to You.
Deliver me from this Strongman
I needed the healing touch of the Savior's hand
To take away the Silence and the Shame
The Fear that came with keeping secrets
And the Blame
Lord, take away the Hurt and the Pain
Let me see the worth in myself again
And give me a heart of forgiveness
That I might be a living witness
A walking weapon of warfare and deliverance
For the salvation of souls
From the crown of my head to the tip of my toes
I'm empowered to Courageously Overthrow and Dethrone the
Enemy
And every demonic spirit or entity
That tries to rear its ugly head against me.
I'm a warrior 4 The KINGDOM!

In a league of Spiritual Beasts that spit FIYA in every place we meet!!!
Let our feet STOMP on new ground
This is a spiritual war we wage
AND WE GONE SHAKE THE FOUNDATIONS WITH PRAISE!

Gorilla Warfare

Metaphorically speaking...
This piece is a heat seeking missile
Aimed at your cerebral cortex,
Filling the evil vortex
Of the black hole that sits in your soul...
That void left from when you were six years old,
When darkness of night tried to suck the light outcha.
Like mouth to mouth in reverse...
It inhaled your blessings and blew out a curse
Like John Coffey in the Green Mile,
Meanwhile...
First impressions of sin soaked confessions
Spoke in your spirit so only your inner man could hear it,
Cause the devil never saw you as a child.
Think on that for a while...
Ever since I came into the game,
He been trying to keep me out of the Book of Names.
Like moths to a flame
Principalities came and set wickedness in high places
To battle against my name,
Cause we wrestle not against flesh and blood.
These demons of darkness never wanted me to spark this
Spiritually gifted, lyrically lifted written remark...
This war of the tongue.
Ever fearful for what I would become,
The devil calls me an Army of One!

A Spiritual Beast 4 The KINGDOM!
A weapon of War, a symbol of Freedom!
We bring 'um back from the gates of jail
To escape the awaits of hell...
Speaking blessings over their lives
Through the lessons we tell.
These spoken testimonies of brokenness.
A token of nothing less
Than Jesus' destiny manifested in me
Cause He resurrected perfected
And I inherited He
And we can either fight or pray...
I'm a warrior for the King.
A weapon of praise whenever I sing...
And I speak release into your hearing.

FROM A PRODIGAL SON

My Testimony Part 1

I have yet to reach mid-life, but the crises I face on a daily basis reverberate in places that remind me of hard times. Dark times race through my mind... Memories of moments when I walked away from God. I thought to stay was hard, but never knew how much harder it would be to return. Like lost souls, I yearn to come home to a resting place. My nesting place is my Blessed-in place. The Sanctuary from whence I came. My Cup bears my Father's name and I'm reminded of it daily. Lord, let this cup pass from me but... Not my will, Thy will be Destiny. I've prayed sometimes... In the corners of my mind dark days I find... where I counted this calling as a curse... and I couldn't figure which was worst, my walking away or His continually calling me. How fallen is he? Like an angel who led Praise, now refusing to sing. Unsung so many ways, now silent is he. Lost one so many days, now come unto me... I keep hearing him call, but my Prodigal Mind keeps me against a wall and I lay splayed by a blade called The Word upon my soul... in my silence he casts scripture upon me like stones, and I am bruised by each and every one. Tongue lashes whip at my flesh, killing a carnal me... filling me spiritually until I AM become what Word would have of me. Now, my days upon this earth may not be long... so let not the stage of life I'm in be wrong. Let me raise up. Send my Praise up... see me high and lifted in a place called Cup. Set my gifted spirit free when praise pours out of me and I AM again come Home. Strengthen my Brother when I no longer roam, but AM returned to my rightful place. My write full page in this stage of life wasn't written by me. I walk not in my own authority, but AM led down lighted pathways. Righted my long strays... my lost days in darkness are become clear. Father draw me near. To Thee, let me continually remain dear. Let not reprobate take shape in my mind. Guide me through my trying times. Let my steps be ordered for my son's and daughter's sake. So they won't have to make the mistakes I make. Trying to escape the traps he baits with the sin that tempts my soul. This war is as old as time... His Story unfolds as mine... Victory is told in His story when He rose in three days Divine. By God's design, purpose was birthed in me... Predestinated, created He praise in me. Amazingly, through my tests and trials He carried me miles. When I look back at the footprints in my sand, I smile. He made beaches of my desert places... My life's oasis springs from a well that'll never run dry... and I will forever cry How Great! Never late, is Our God. He is always right on time. So, at this stage of life where I'm... I Press... towards the mark... for the prize... of the high calling... and I press towards the sound of My Calling. I'm blessed through my pressing and if somehow others are blessed through my call, then let my testimony tell it all. I AM a prodigal son, but when my race is run, my Father's face will be the one to tell me well done...

I shall return Home.

Spoken to My Broken Heart
My Testimony Part 2

Everyone has a word, but none has one I haven't heard and my heart is still the same...Come one, speak healing to my pain cause I haven't got over it yet. We don't speak on what was taken, just on what was left. "D'ever a hearTlesS liar" left my heart to die in pain. I suppose this was my Passion cause it was done in God's name, and I have never felt so crucified. I hung my head and died inside and The Spirit no longer lived in me... and all I had to give in me slipped away in my grief. And you offered me no relief and my days became the blackest nights. And I embraced a darker life... And my LIVE revealed itself in the mirror... and I no longer had a fear of EVIL, but took up solace in shadowy places... If I can't escape this... void in space this... black hole in my soul, then I must make this... sorrow my dwelling place. Cover my face in ash and sit Indian style... sift through cinders for a while... Rent my cloak and arose like a Phoenix in the wild. Dare, Sir, I render my heart unto sorrow? Never surrender... I borrowed from Rage and hardened my heart to love's ways. Where is my healing? Speak to my feelings? Don't waste your time... feelings change. That's why I smolder my emotions... elevate my game... and never again to you mention her name. I wreak havoc on hearts... Black Angel in flight... How many lost in the night have I slain? Where was your Light when I whispered to their pain? "No one has to know... you don't have to hurt again. Come with me, my yoke is easy and my burden light. You don't have to fear the Dark when you embrace the Night."

This flame once flickered as cloven tongues when The Spirit comes, until Pain reigned in his life. When rain came it was like 40 days without light and 40 nights. And it flooded my soul... the levees couldn't hold, so released my grief in tears for years. Unable to swim a sea of sorrow or swallow an ocean... my tomorrows drowned in my emotion till I found the strength to love again. Took hold of another hand... had to let go the first. Which was worse, holding on or letting go? I still don't know, maybe I never will... But from what I can tell... it was worth the loss. Love was worth the cost and it cost me everything. But it taught me that I had the ability to abundantly love again. Loss didn't have to harden me... though it left a part of me void and without form, I shape like pottery. I mold like clay in The Potter's hands. He can break me and reshape me to be used once again... and I become a vessel of Love. I pour like water from heaven above and saturate 10,000 lakes. I'll conquer darkness again if that's what it takes to walk in high places and I shall not be moved. Hear in my praise... it's what I do. And be saved by the Word of this testimony. Heartbroken, hurt, depressed and lonely no longer live here. I walk not in a spirit of fear, but in the Power of His might over my life. Delight myself in His ways... and bleed the ink of my soul upon this page. My testimony is so much more than my own. My life has been places you've never known, but what He imparts in me... I impart in thee... and we in part become spiritually connected. My heart was affected to spread love like wildfires. As I write He gives me the desires to inspire you. This Gift to me was true before I begun... Now it's the testimony of a Prodigal Son.

My Prodigal Testimony

First Spoken at Power of the Tongue Café
This is not a performance.
This is not for your entertainment or listening pleasure.
This is not a test...
This is not what you would typically expect of me.
This is a testimony...
A confess as only I can.
Spoken by what used to be only a broken man.
A token of a broken stand
A fallen stood.
Why do I do evil, when I would to do good?
Lord why... do You keep calling my name?
Why can't I live the life of just an ordinary man?
See, these are questions that I use-ta' ask,
But use-ta' is the past...
And use-ta' wouldn't use-ta' let me last,
So I have no USE for use-ta' anymore.
There use-ta' be a time where I battled...
But now I WAR!
There use-ta' be a time when I struggled...
But now I don't.
I've stumbled,
And I'm not saying that I won't...
But I CAN'T be persuaded anymore.
I'm not playing anymore.
I'm not tip-toeing around the devils door.

Cause the devil got happy when I fell back.
I had to tell him... Get back!
It's just a set back...
I stepped back
Took a look at myself again to see who I REALLY am...
Raised Praise to the God of my life!
I'M BACK IN!
He should've killed me when he had the chance...
I AINT PLAYIN' NO MORE!
I'M MUCH STRONGER NOW... MY SOUL IS SET FOR WAR!
CAUSE I FOUGHT THE SAME BATTLE TOO MANY TIMES TO GAIN THE SAME GROUND
ITS TIME TO ADVANCE BEHIND ENEMY LINES AND CLAIM NEW FOUND NATIONS...
LAZARUS PLACES...
AND TAKE HOLD OF EVERY SOUL THAT GOD TOLD ME COULD BE TAKEN!
ITS A NEW DAY!
I'm moving forward in authority
Professing every word and lesson God's afforded me...
This ain't a standoff.
It's a COMMAND-OFF!
I took the handoff... now it's time to go to WAR!
And I won't be fooled by my enemy...
Though he be a liar and a cheat.
I know the war that's set before me.

And I already have the VICTORY!
IF GOD BE FOR ME... THEN WHO CAN BE AGAINST ME!?
WHO BE THEY TO FENCE ME?
I WAR TO SET CAPTIVES FREE...
FOR NO SHACKLES HOLD ME NOW.
THAT BREAKTHROUGH PRAISE RAISED ME SOMEHOW!
It took a little while...
My Dark wasn't trying to find The Light.
I had to PRAISE the Darkness out of my Night
So my LIFE could see Brighter days.
HIS ways are not our ways...
He had to break me down to take me to a higher place.
But broke me and remolded me.
Holded me enfolded...
HE said, BEHOLD, IS HE ALL THAT I SAID HE WOULD BE...
AND MY WORD SHALL NOT RETURN UNTO ME VOID.
Spoke into my Destiny before my conception HE...
Ordained me a Weapon for the Lord.
A Dragon Slayer!
A Fire Breathing Prayer!
A Yielding Shield of Faith, Hands Layer!
A Whole Armor Bearer!
A Wearer of Robe and Crown!
And when PRAISE goes UP... HE REIGNS DOWN!
Anointed me Appointed me a King and a Priest.
My Sword and Cross both slay the beast.

HIS Word and HIS Love...
HIS Power and HIS Blood...
And if by our Testimonies, we shall overcome
Then I will Testify until the day I DIE!
HE Saved me!
The light HE gave me will shine like a beacon for all to see...
For I AM AN INSTRUMENT OF PRAISE!
A WEAPON OF WAR!
I CAN'T BE DEFEATED ANYMORE...
AND I WON'T QUIT!!!
YOU KNEW THE DAY WAS COMING... AND THIS IS IT!!!
AND WE ABOUT TO SET THE CHURCH ON FIRE!
IF IT AIN'T SUPPOSED TO BE HERE LET IT BURN...
DEVIL BEWARE,
THE PRODIGAL SON'S RETURNED!

SIX WORDS... 8/31

Predestined Creation...
Dominion, Salvation and Eternity

PERFECT DAYS

They say not every day will be perfect,
But I disagree
Because every day is a perfect opportunity
Perfectly created
But I can mess it up if choose to.
Who's to...
Say I can't have a perfect day?
It just so happens that I like the rain...
So who's to blame for your cloudy days?
When you can't see rays of hope and skies of blue
Is not a rainy day a blessing too?
Because truthfully we need the rain
To wash away some of the stains of our iniquities
To cleanse the streets of our filth and discarded debris
When brokenheartedly
I stood and watched the rain fall
So all... couldn't see my tears
But I had been brokenhearted for years
I came to love the rain...

Winds blow
And there's a cold feel to my soul
A distant chill and I'm sickening...
My spirit's ill and I'm listening to my enemy
Come, Shekinah rain and quicken me
Like a warm flood to my soul...

Rain manna down from heaven
Feed me till I want no more
Your provision is all I'm thirsting for
Send the rains

Let them pour over me like
Cascades from Irish Springs...
Calgon to take me away
Till Dawn brings a new day...

And it's perfect

A Way Out of Darkness

I took a journey by my lonesome self
No shelter could I find
No peace for my wandering mind...
And No comfort
My soul was cold all the time.
My days were cloudy and my way was unclear
I couldn't focus
Every glimmer of hope would disappear.
And the enemy was a friend-a-me...
He paid attention to the lonely condition
Of my state of mind
He baited a weighted line like a great deceiver
And I fell for her every time; hook, line and sinker.
And he just kept reeling me in
There goes that feeling again
I'm too far gone to get back home now.
My lost soul roams now...
I'm all alone now.
These thoughts like black lace he began to weave

He fishes from the deep
Casting nets of deceit upon the shores of your soul
To entangle you and pull you out to sea...
His snares are often beautiful lies and trickery
Disguised to steal your time.
His plan is to snare your beautiful mind

And strangle you with chaos and confusion
Disillusion you with lust for what you consider loves sake
Abuse your trust until your love turns to hate
And leave you lost in a reprobate state of mind.
Drowning in loneliness
Depressed and heartbroken in hopelessness
Confessed but misspoken
A careless guest of loves token and lust's deceit.
For a token of lust was just loves defeat.
Had me defeated and mistreated me repeatedly
So I then began to abuse myself
Until my hurt grew into hurting someone else
Someone I could use just as much as he was using me
And I embraced lust, fornication and adultery
Forsaken all morality for sexuality and material gains...
I was in spiritual chains
In bondage to a beast who wouldn't let go of me.
He molested my mentality
Perverted my heart
And raped me until I embraced the dark...
And hid myself inside my shame
But I could hear Jesus calling my name...
I could still hear Him calling me...
Lord, as messed up as I am,
What could You want with me...
What could You possibly see?
And he said...

Prodigal Son come back to me
You are the one that my heart seeks
Whatever you've done...
I cast it out of my memory
Though there be many in my house
It's still empty without
My Prodigal Son...
And the tears began to run...
My knees began to bend
And I asked Jesus to walk with me again
And break the stronghold the devil had on my soul
So that I could once again be used of Him.
And He renewed in me a Praise
One for which I raise my voice and say Hallelujah!
My life... I'll give it to You every day!
Thank you Lord for making a way out of sin
For taking the hurt and bringing the shame to an end.
For breaking the chains the devil had me bound in.
So that I can, now, say unto them...
Be mindful of your heart and others intentions...
Be lovers of God and His ambitions for your soul.
You make a perfect pair.
Behold... A winning combination
When you develop a true relationship with God.
It's never too late to start.
You ain't ever too far gone to come back home.

Don't believe the lies the devil tries to tell...
He knows what you'll buy cause he's watched you well...
And he'll sell you anything...
Just to get you to pay the cost.
His ultimate goal is your soul be lost...
So, let Jesus be your compass...
A lamp unto your feet

You'll find direction in every word He speaks.
His arms are always open
He's always hoping for your safe return...
Let Past trials and tribulations be lessons learned
Turn tests into testimony.
Confessions into blessings for someone else
Who might be dealing with the same feeling that you felt.
How I dealt might help you
Get through what you're going through.
When I felt I had nothing else left to lose... I praised.
Though I never should have waited that long...
See... When you're going through the key is to keep pressing on...
Keep praising... Praise Him through every situation.
Your elevation is dependent upon your praise.
Hallelujah is the highest.
When I'm low, I wanna go as high as I can...
So I've learned to lift up both hands...
And HALLELUJAH in the highest! All praise to Jesus name

Through Christ my life will never be the same...
This is a chance for change; a moment of divine opportunity
Don't be deceived into believing you have immunity.
Receive Christ... make a change... rededicate your life.
Let Him make your wrongs ways right.
Let Him order your steps... He loves you just like you never left...
Let Him be your Souls Salvation.
You and Jesus... a winning combination.

INDEX OF FIRST LINES

Her beauty has never impeded me.
Her Beauty's captured
Hidden emotions
I am a victim of love
I am more than the sum of my parts.
I can imagine His hands carefully molding the clay
I could erase all the mistakes we'd ever make
I have a propensity for pondering
I hear the sound in your voice when you speak to me.
I keep hearing… "You're not made for material gains…
I remember those back-in-the-days.
I sit here in silence pining for words to say to you…
I slept through the night
I think best in ebony, but indigo will do
I took a journey by my lonesome self
I understand that you've been hurt in the past,
I used to be grimy but now I'm grizzly
I used to follow music
I want to paint a picture for you
I woke up this morning feeling some kind of way
I would that life could never end
I would walk you through weathered storms
I write in spite of pain…
I write like my life depended on it
I'm a child of soul music…
I'm guilty

I'm not ready to deal with another person's insecurities.
I'm sick and tired...
I'm sick of being disciplined
I'm so sick of the hypocrisy
If I could bottle it up and keep it forever
If I could draw you a map of the eight square inner city
If I could write a letter to my younger self
If poetry teaches us one thing
If waterfalls of tears
In folded arms you choose to
Is it just me
It's a long way down from here.
It's been a long time since I put pen to line,
It's been so long since words were spoken between us.
It's not news that you're no good for me.
I've watched sunsets and sunrises
Lackadaisical ways
Laying in my arms...
Like a river, run to me
Like feathers released on a breeze,
Lord, I thirst for thee
Lord, let me hide myself in thee
Me and this jones go way back
Metaphorically speaking...
Minister Mother Daughter Sister Friend...
My mind... Made to turn the page

My neighborhood was a jewel to me.
My Soul yet so weeps
My teary eyed...
Not for the sake of having something to say
Now "we" prefer our faces be looked upon independently
Now persuaded I
Now some say He's marvelous
One could exist in such a place as this
Our Father, which art in heaven
Passed the place of gracefully, these days hastily
Pushing against the wind seems to be a theme for me
Remember that time when we were kids
Remember your first pet?
Rewind these dreams and scenes that play over again in my mind
She...
She carries me
Silverback Gorilla Warfare General of the troop
Snap, crackle, pop...
So this piece....
Some days are stranger than others
Spittin' watermelon seeds
Sweet angelic being...
Taken the road less traveled
Teach me how to hold you...
There were those days growing up
There would be wood where their noses grow

There's a rhythm in the distance
These tears comfort me.
They call me Brother
They said it could never be done
They say not every day will be perfect
This is a soulful moan.
Tie your shoes... Tuck your shirt in...
Till We Meet Again
Times ticking
Today came a blessing in her pressing onward
Troubles came today
We once wed to be
We used to be like nobody's business...
Welcome to real life.
When wonderings have left me all alone
Will you be my lover?
Yeah, you be that Chris Rock in Vanity Fair,
You move through me
You took me riding in a rocket

Printed in the United States
By Bookmasters